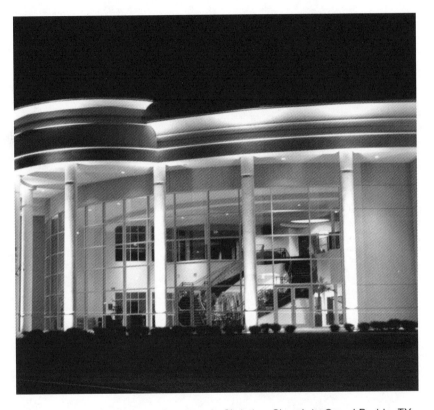

Pictures in this book are of Crossroads Christian Church in Grand Prairie, TX, where Barry Cameron is the Senior Pastor.

What Leaders Are Saying About
The ABCs of Financial Freedom

"Our church completed a financial series using Barry Cameron's book entitled, *The ABCs of Financial Freedom.* We gave out 5,000 copies to our members and also used the book as a basis for small group discussion as well as our sermon series. The result exceeded by far anything we have ever done in trying to raise the level of giving in our church. We had over 1,300 people sign up to tithe for the first time. Our giving increased by 45% in the first month. The most important thing that happened was the way it challenged our people to trust God with their finances and move to a deeper level of commitment. Barry's message wrapping up the series was icing on the cake and tied the whole series together. The extra resources we are receiving will enable our church to get out of debt quicker and expand our ministry around the world. I would highly recommend this to your church. If you have any concerns or questions, please feel free to give me a call."

Dr. Don Wilson, Senior Pastor
Christ's Church of the Valley
Peoria, AZ

"Barry L. Cameron is respected as an extraordinary church builder and preacher. This book is a testimony to his giftedness as a writer. Barry is a cowboy that has been on the ranch. He's been there and done that. It is written in a language easily understood. He gives a clear picture of his personal struggles and a straightforward explanation of what God says about money and our use of it. I'm certain Barry will be on the hit list of the credit card industry. However, I believe he will be fondly remembered as a no-holds-barred writer who encouraged us to be honest with God and ourselves. If and when this happens, we can joyfully say, 'Free at last, free at last, praise God, I'm free at last.'"

Wayne B. Smith, founding Pastor
Southland Christian Church
Lexington, KY

"God's stewardship principles aren't complicated. They are as simple as ABC. But simple doesn't always mean easy. In fact, God's stewardship principles are proving difficult to live by for most of us in our "debt is normal, saving is an afterthought, and God wants what?!" culture. We need great information, sure. But more than that, we need motivation that leads to transformation and that's what our church received with Barry Cameron and *The ABCs of Financial Freedom*. By telling the story of how he applied *The ABCs* in his own life, Barry motivated the people of our church to take action to get out of debt, build wealth through savings, and give God their best. All of our people were affected by *The ABCs*. One family in our church said it best. They have drastically improved their financial situation, too: "Those who don't understand the power of compounding interest, pay it, those who understand the power, earn it!"

Dave Dummitt, Pastor
242 Community Church
Brighton, MI

"The impact Barry had on our church will be felt for generations to come. He is clear, charismatic and compelling; but most importantly, he is biblical! *The ABC's* weekend catalyzed both gratitude and opportunity. Rather than reminding us of another difficult obligation, Barry opened our eyes to God's desire to partner with us and empower us to both be blessed and be a blessing to the world. I highly recommend that you invite Barry for a life-changing weekend of discovery concerning the transformational power of godly stewardship. You will not be disappointed!"

Jeff Vines, Pastor
Christ's Church of the Valley
San Dimas, CA

"Our church went through *The ABC's* series in early 2013. We had dozens of families commit to debt-free living and to tithing for the first time. Our weekly offerings have stayed significantly higher ever since. Now when we speak each week of 'tithes and offerings,' everyone knows what we mean. We also give away *The ABCs of Financial Freedom* to every new member so all members will continue to be on the same page in our pursuit of debt-free living and stewardship of God's resources. I highly recommend *The ABCs of Financial Freedom*."

Rusty Russell, Lead Pastor
New Day Christian Church
Port Charlotte, FL

"Barry Cameron fulfills his twin callings of prophet [preacher] and pastor in his new book entitled, *The ABCs of Financial Freedom*. He knows how to afflict the comfortable and comfort the afflicted on this topic. And do we ever need it! A few of us need someone to get in our face and confront our selfishness and materialism. Others of us need someone to give us hope and a strategy for recovery. This book has both components. And, of course, good Bible teaching on this subject is especially enlightening and energizing.

There is so much from both secular society and even the Christian community on this topic that is blatantly self-serving. It is refreshing to finally read something that is thoroughly biblical, practical and helpful. What Larry Burkett provides from the perspective of a Christian financial planner, Barry Cameron contributes from the vantage point of a megachurch pastor. The theology is solid. The tone is urgent. The appeal is popular. The language is contemporary. The illustrations are fresh. The book is not just readable, it is compelling. Don't pick it up if you have things to do. You will be quickly hooked by its sermonic impact. You won't want to put it down. This book should be required reading for any Christian who wants to practice responsible stewardship of our life and living."

Ken Idleman, Senior Pastor
Crossroads Christian Church
Evansville, IN

"My friend, Barry Cameron, is a wonderful communicator and practitioner of biblically-based financial counsel. He knows the way, goes the way, and in this helpful book, shows the way to financial freedom. Many people in our congregation have experienced authentic money makeovers because they have put into practice the wisdom outlined in Barry's book. Of course, Barry would be the first to say that everything good he has to share about money comes from *the* Book. If you ever have the opportunity to hear Barry teach in person on this subject, don't miss it. Do what you need to do get there. Until then, read this book and begin dreaming of what it feels like to have no debt outstanding except the continuing debt of love. Imagine being able to be generous on every occasion. It can happen. It did for Barry. It has for many that have taken seriously what Barry advocates in these pages. It can for you, too."

John Hampton, Senior Pastor
Journey Christian Church
Apopka, FL

"We did *The ABCs of Financial Freedom*. The emphasis completely moved from the church's need or personal need to a matter of Lordship. We realized that the capital campaigns of our past, while useful, actually moved people toward church needs and away from tithing as a biblically taught expression of Lordship. Our church began to understand debt as an obstacle that prevented us from experiencing Lordship creating an environment of rebellion. *The ABCs* helped us to remove the debt obstacle and replace it with the obedience of tithing.

The result? Peace. Our families realized the peace that flows out of the obedience of Lordship. Peace in our priorities, our choices, and our future. We recognized that God has always provided for both our individual needs and our needs as a church; we were just not realizing it because we were not releasing it. We didn't need another catchy 3-year campagn ... we needed to trust God and let Him have His way. Our church giving has doubled, our church debt is going away, our baptisms have doubled, and we are experiencing the provision of God around every corner! While our nation is in turmoil over health care, for the first time, our church provides full health care and retirement. I look on the faces of our staff and our members and I see an ever-widening sense of peace living in obedience under the care and provision of our Lord!"

Jerry Harris, Pastor
The Crossing
Quincy, IL

"I've been a pastor long enough to know that churches are always looking for new and effective ways to challenge their people to deeper levels of discipleship knowing that a deeper commitment not only enriches and blesses their lives, but also benefits the church's overall mission to reach lost people. *The ABCs of Financial Freedom* is a resource that does just that.

When we went through *The ABCs*, our people were impacted in a significant way. Not only did our weekly offerings increase by almost 40%, but we developed a greater church-wide understanding that stewardship is Lordship, and the way we handle God's money reveals a lot about our faith. Because of that I have encouraged pastors all around the country to make *The ABCs* a part of their preaching plan. God is literally using this resource to change lives, change churches and change the world."

Chris Philbeck, Pastor
Mount Pleasant Christian Church
Greenwood, IN

"It always amazes me that after challenging our people constantly to trust and depend upon God, they so quickly place blame for a lack of giving in the church on leadership. Barry Cameron's *ABCs of Financial Freedom* material was an answer to many of my late night prayers. The material reinforced the fact that the church today is not struggling with a lack of resources. It is struggling with a lack of obedience and faithfulness. We were amazed at both the immediate jump in our giving, as well as how the high level of giving was sustained."

Tim Winters, Executive Pastor
Shepherd of the Hills Church
Porter Ranch, CA

"The principles in *The ABCs of Financial Freedom* are biblical and life changing. In a time when so many people are drowning in foolish debt, *The ABCs* are a desperately needed lifeline. I have taught these principles again and again to my congregation with amazing results!"

Steve Bond, Senior Pastor
Summit Christian Church,
Sparks, NV

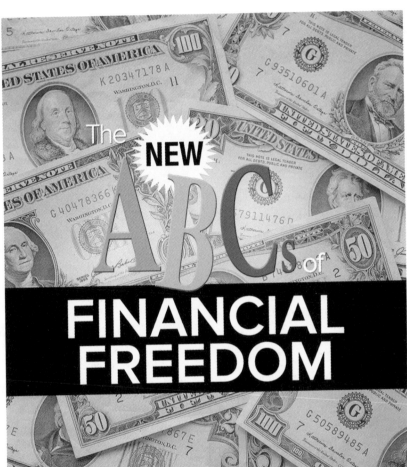

The NEW ABCs of

FINANCIAL FREEDOM

BARRY L. CAMERON

The New ABCs of Financial Freedom

Copyright © 2015 by Barry L. Cameron

College Press Publishing Company
www.collegepress.com

First Printing 2001

International Standard Book Number: 978-0-89900-958-2

The Library of Congress has catalogued an earlier printing as follows:

Library of Congress Cataloging-in-Publication Data

Cameron, Barry L. (Barry Lee), 1955-
    The A, B, C's of financial success / Barry L. Cameron.
      p. cm.
    Includes bibliographical references.
    ISBN 0-89900-824-0 (pbk.)
    1. Finance, Personal—Religious aspects—Christianity. I. Title.
HG179.C3145 2001
332.024—dc21

                        2001047689

DEDICATION

To Janis, Katie, Matt and Kelli,
for sharing the vision and making the sacrifices
so we could be debt free.

To the Crossroads Christian Church family,
the most generous church in America.

ACKNOWLEDGMENTS

My special thanks to our wonderful church family at Crossroads for putting these principles into practice and giving generously so our church could become debt free.

To Mel Dietz, my friend and our Executive Pastor, who is a genius when it comes to managing and administrating a church.

To Vicki Dietz, my friend and my administrative assistant, who for more than thirty years has made me look much better than I am.

TABLE OF CONTENTS

FOREWORD

I've read lots of books in my lifetime, but when it comes to a book with uniqueness and immediate impact, I can't remember one that has made such an impression on me, and tens of thousands of others as well.

The simple story of how Barry Cameron got his family and his church completely out of debt is amazing in and of itself. The impact that story has had on the lives of people here in America and around the world is, in a word, astounding. I met Barry Cameron and saw his church for the first time in October, 2000, when the church was running 1,600. Today, they average over 6,000 in morning worship on a completely debt free, 150-acre campus.

I know of no single person that has Barry's credibility. The credibility of his church, Crossroads Christian Church in Grand Prairie, Texas, is also unparalleled. I know of no church that has done what they have done or is doing what they are doing.

On the day they broke ground for their new campus, October 6, 2002, they gave a check for $200,000.00 to help start STADIA, a brand new church planting organization. On November 6, 2012, the day they began raising funds for their new children's building, they gave over $315,000.00 to build a new wing for a hospital in Damoh, India, as well as a new youth center on the campus of CICM (Central India Christian Mission) there.

In November of 2013, they broke ground for a new 75,000 sq. ft. children's building that was already paid for and are raising another $15 million now to build a new 75,000 sq. ft. youth building. Both facilities completely financed with cash.

Over the past decade I've had a front row seat watching Barry and his son, Matt, share these principles in over 125 churches for ABC's weekends and witnessed thousands of people's lives being changed forever. Families and individuals learning to trust God with their finances, cutting up credit cards, paying off debts, being able to burn their mortgages and get completely debt free.

The impact on the Kingdom has been enormous. Individuals and entire families changed forever. Churches having resources to move more money into ministry and missions.

There is no better book to read if you want to discover the joy of being debt free than *The ABCs of Financial Freedom*. It will generate a higher yield than any investment advisor can guarantee. You'll find yourself wanting to share it with your friends. Parents, it's the perfect primer for helping your children and teenagers get started on the road to financial freedom. Pastors, you're going to want every leader and member of your church to read this book.

This book takes the timeless truths of Scripture and makes it as easy as A, B, C to understand and apply, so all of us can achieve financial freedom.

Enjoy!

Douglas J. Crozier, CEO
The Solomon Foundation
Englewood, CO

INTRODUCTION

One of the worst hostage crises in American history took place on November 4, 1979, when a group of Iranian militants stormed the U.S. Embassy in Tehran. After initially taking close to 70 hostages they wound up keeping 52 people in captivity for a period of 444 days. The crisis ended on January 20, 1981, minutes after the inauguration of Ronald Reagan as the 40th President of the United States. I'll never forget the looks on the faces of those former captives once they were *FREE*.

While that hostage crisis was bad, it doesn't come close to representing the worst hostage crisis in our country's history. That designation belongs to the current crisis in America where millions of people are being held hostage by debt. It's a crisis of cataclysmic proportions, with people in completely frustrating, financial captivity – unable to do what they want to do because they're enslaved – having to make payments for what they've already done.

Our family was set *FREE* from that debt crisis on November 15, 2001. I'll never forget the day or the feeling I experienced making the final payment on the mortgage for our home, declaring our family's financial independence. This book is about our experience and the principles we applied from God's Word that enabled us to finally enjoy genuine *financial freedom*.

Christians ought to be the best money managers on the planet, and churches ought to be the best-run institutions when it comes to the subject of finances. Unfortunately, in most cases, we aren't.

Several things are obvious: *One*, the majority of Christians, like the majority of those who are unchurched, are in serious debt and unnecessarily struggling with their finances on a week-to-week basis. *Two*, we're not nearly as good at managing our money and resources as we think we are. *Three*, churches need to do a better job practicing the principles of God's Word in their finances, enabling them to be better equipped and better able to teach on money and financial issues to help their people. *Four*, we aren't even coming close to our potential when it comes to financial stewardship.

This book is about changing all that. My prayer is that reading this book will become one of the best investments you've ever made, that it will pay dividends for the rest of your life and ...

... you can experience genuine *Financial Freedom!*

Barry L. Cameron, Senior Pastor
Crossroads Christian Church
Grand Prairie, Texas

FROM THE
GOOD FILE
Simple ideas to encourage you to
GET OUT OF DEBT

Have you ever stopped to think what it would be like to be completely DEBT FREE? A lot of people live their entire lives thinking and believing it would be impossible for them to ever achieve the goal of being debt free. But, what if it weren't? (And it isn't! Being debt free is within reach of **anyone** who **wants** to reach that goal.)

What if it were possible for **you** to be totally and completely DEBT FREE? Think about it! Can you imagine what you could do?

Solomon wrote in Proverbs, "Where there is no vision, the people perish" (29:18, KJV). He also wrote, "As a man thinks in his heart, so is he" (23:7, NKJV). So, if having a vision and having the right thinking is that important, maybe you and I should do some Christ-centered vision casting of our own and start thinking about what we could do if we were totally debt free.

Here are just a few suggestions to help you get started:

1. You would be free to give to God and the church like you always wanted to.
2. You could start doing whatever you want with your money. (Imagine more money than bills!)
3. You would have no outstanding debts except that continuing debt to love one another.
4. You could put money in savings and earn lots of interest for a change instead of paying it.
5. You could help your immediate and extended family.
6. You could finally have that "dream" vacation.
7. You could fix things around your house or even get a new one.
8. You could get new furniture or a new vehicle.

9. You could surprise people with secret acts of kindness and generosity.

10. You could do almost anything you can imagine.

Action Plans

Now, here's the point. If we don't ***think*** we can be debt free, we never will be. But if all we do is think about it and dream about it and don't start DOING SOMETHING about it, it won't happen.

So, take some G.O.O.D. advice: 1) sit down and make out a ***wish*** list of all the things you'd like to do once you're debt free. Then, 2) make a list of all the things you ***need*** to do in order to get debt free. Once you've done that, get to work on list #2 (the list of things you need to do). And, each week and each month, as you are able to check something off your "to do" list, you are one step closer to being able to check things off list #1 ... and seeing your dreams come true!

CHAPTER 1

ATTITUDE

"The greatest discovery of my generation is that a human being can alter his life by altering his attitude."
—William James

SECRET SANTA

You may not know his name; nobody did; and that's just the way he wanted it. But you'll never forget what I'm about to tell you. They called him "Secret Santa," and the week before Christmas in 1999 he handed out $85,000 in $100 bills to unsuspecting people on the streets of Kansas City.

The story actually begins in 1971, in Houston, Mississippi, a small county seat town. The man who would become Secret Santa was then a young salesman. Every week his employer would send him a paycheck and pay rent on a small office and a room at a local motel. But one day the employer went out of business and failed to tell the young man. After losing his motel room for nonpayment, the young man slept in his car for eight nights. He kept waiting for a paycheck that never arrived. Out of gas and money, he turned to a local church for assistance. The person who supervised the fund to help the poor was gone the day he inquired. The next morning he walked into the Dixie Diner, a small brick café around the corner from Walgreen's in Houston, Mississippi. Having not eaten for two days, he ordered a huge breakfast and slowly sipped coffee refills, wondering how he could escape without paying. Finally, he pretended to lose his wallet. The owner, who was also the cook, waiter, and cashier, lifted a countertop door and walked behind the young man's leather-covered stool, reached toward the floor, and acted as if he picked something up. "You must have dropped this," the owner said, handing the young man $20. The young salesman's heart was pounding as he paid, left a tip, raced outside and pushed his car to a gas station before fleeing. As he drove away, he thought about how fortunate he was. Suddenly it occurred to him that no one had dropped that money. The man behind the counter knew he was in trouble and helped him in a way that allowed him to keep his dignity. "If I'm ever in a position to help other people," he told himself, "that's what I'm going to do."

Later that year the young salesman rode a Greyhound bus to Kansas City where he found a sales job and continued living from paycheck to paycheck. He became a wealthy Jackson County businessman who regularly handed out $50,000 or more during each of his Christmas campaigns, which he did for over 26 years. In 2000, Secret Santa located the Mississippi diner owner, Mr. Ted Horn. He told Mr. Horn he was doing research on Secret Santa and wanted to come down and meet him. When they met, Mr. Horn said he always wanted to meet Secret Santa himself because he remembered the guy and remembered the $20. "It was in my diner where it happened," he said. "I know, Mr. Horn," Secret Santa revealed, "I was that young salesman."

"By the way, what do you reckon that $20 bill is worth today? Do you know how to figure net present value? I had somebody figure that for me." Before Secret Santa could tell Horn the answer, which was about $120, Horn gave a response that fit right into Secret Santa's plans. He said, "Well, to me that $20 bill then was probably like $10,000 to you today." "Funny

you should say that," Secret Santa replied as he pu.
envelope full of $100 bills with a strap of paper around ا
$10,000. "You don't have to do this," Horn said softl,
wanted to," Secret Santa replied. "You never know what o ..c little
act of kindness will do for somebody. It can change their whole
life. You sure changed mine."[1]

In November of 2006, Secret Santa died from esophageal
cancer that had spread to his liver. When he died, the world
discovered 58-year-old Larry Stewart had been the man who
changed so many lives.

You are holding in your hands a life-changing book, *The
ABCs of Financial Freedom*. Next to the Bible it might be the
most important book you've ever read because of the principles
you're going to learn. In fact, it's very possible you will look back
on this book and realize it was one of the greatest things that ever
happened to you. I believe, for some people, they'll look back and
say, "You know what, that book was worth a million dollars to
me." It might as well be you.

So let's get started.

INTEREST NOT SO INTERESTING

The average person doesn't really believe he has a problem
when it comes to finances. He really doesn't. As long as he's
making monthly payments on time, as long as he has some mad
money he can play with each week, as long as he can continue to
feed and satisfy those occasional indulgences from time to time,
he erroneously believes things are just fine. Unfortunately he's
like the alcoholic, the drug addict, the gambler, or the person
addicted to pornography who says, "I don't have a problem." But
the truth is, the average American has a major problem when it
comes to money, Christians included. They are horribly in debt,
miserable managers of their money, and gullible beyond belief

when it comes to buying things on credit. Can I share a simple principle with you? If you're paying interest on anything, regardless of the great interest rate you may have gotten or the low monthly payment; if you are paying interest on anything, are you ready for this? YOU ARE LOSING MONEY.

In fact, when you see the word "interest," if you visualize two words in huge, gigantic letters as if they were written in the sky, "SOMEBODY ELSE," that will help you better comprehend the principle. Why? Because that's exactly what happens every time you're paying interest. SOMEBODY ELSE is getting rich off YOUR money. Yet so many people say, "Well, you know, we got a great interest rate." Or, "Luckily I got the same low monthly payment on this car that I had on my last one."

In 1999, Christian financial expert, Larry Burkett, said, "Christians are now paying nearly 10% of our income every year in interest alone. And yet we give only 2% back to God."[2] In the years since, people are paying even more of their income in interest and giving less to God. So here's the picture. The average Christian in America is miserably over his head in debt and walking in rebellion towards God. We definitely have a problem. But you'd better be reasonably bold and considerably courageous if you attempt to suggest to someone he has a problem with his finances. Why? Because we're very touchy when it comes to our stuff. When it comes to my money and my finances, that's a private matter, and it's none of your business. Isn't that pretty much the way you feel? So if someone suggests we have a problem with our finances, we immediately get defensive and go into denial because none of us want to admit we have a problem.

HARRY TRUMAN VERSUS THE VOLCANO

Do you remember Harry Truman? Not the President. The man who lived on the side of Mount St. Helens in

Washington? I'll never forget the guy. He had 23 cats. (Does that help?) In 1980 he was on Mount St. Helens. TV reporters were interviewing him while the mountain was shaking behind him. Harry's sitting there with his 23 cats and seismologists were saying, "This mountain's gonna blow." Volcanic experts were saying, "This mountain's gonna blow." Harry Truman said, "I don't believe a single one of your experts. I've lived here all my life. I know this old mountain better than anybody else. I'm not going anywhere." And they'd banter back and forth.

I remember his sister on national television (you may remember watching). She pleaded with her brother, "Please, get off this mountain. It's gonna blow." "No, it's not," Harry insisted. "I've lived here all my life. I don't have a problem."

On May 18, 1980, at 8:31 a.m., the mountain blew. It blew with a force 500 times greater than the power of the bomb that was dropped on Hiroshima. Twenty-five hundred feet blew off the top of the mountain. It blackened the sky from Seattle to New York and as far south as Oklahoma.

No one has ever seen a trace of Harry or his 23 cats since.

DECLARING FINANCIAL INDEPENDENCE

Now I'm praying there are no Harry Trumans reading this book. I'm going to assume you want God's wisdom, God's guidance, and God's provision in your life. I'm going to assume you want to be out of debt; and once and for all, as unbelievable as this may seem, to be free from the albatross of financial burdens, bills, and bondage.

I'm going to be intensely practical in these few chapters. I'm going to tell you things you won't believe you've read. I'm going to open up my own home, literally, to you. I'm going to tell you how we handle our finances, how we do our budget, and I'm going to walk you through the mistakes we made.

You're going to be so encouraged by our personal story of finances that you'll say, "Thank you, God, there's hope for all of us." I'm going to share with you the struggles and the successes from our own church. How we went from being a small church, miserably in debt and struggling just to pay bills, to a church reaching thousands and giving millions each year.

So keep reading.

I'm going to tell you who's behind your financial problems, and when you find out it's not you, you're going to be in shock. It'll get your attention. I'm going to tell you how every one of us can be totally and completely out of debt. It's possible for anyone reading this book. In fact, regardless of how much debt you have today, I agree with Larry Burkett, who used to say* in seven years anybody can be out of debt.[3] Anybody. That includes you, and it includes your church.

Our family declared our financial independence in December of 1999. We decided we were sick of debt and developed a strategy so we could be completely debt free in two years. And guess what? It works!

I was in our church prayer room one Sunday morning, and talk about pressure on the preacher. The head of our Prayer Partner Ministry prayed that God would get the preacher out of debt. He knew I'd already made the commitment. My wife and I made the commitment to be totally out of debt in two years. Someone will say, "You must've had a small amount of debt." No, we had a large amount of debt. But we made a commitment before God, altered our lifestyle, and changed the way we did things. We put our whole family on a budget. I was on a budget; my wife was on a budget; our kids were on a budget. In fact, the common line heard around our house during that period when we were getting out of debt was: "Well, that's not in my budget."

We went out to dinner on New Year's Eve and my wife said,

---

*Larry Burkett died in July 2003.

"Now, who's paying for this meal? Is it coming out of my budget or your budget?" It came out of mine. (To be honest, it wasn't worth it.) One night we were ordering pizza and I said, "Now, whose budget is going to cover this?" My wife said, "Oh, I'll take that out of mine."

All of us can be out of debt if we really want to be. But we have to want to. I want to help you "want to." That's why I've written this book. I don't want to hurt you, I want to help you. But if we don't begin with step number one, nothing else we talk about will help. We need to begin with *your attitude* toward money.

YOUR ATTITUDE TOWARD MONEY

Look at the words of David in 1 Chronicles 29:10-14. The Bible says,

David praised the LORD in the presence of the whole assembly, saying
"Praise be to you, O LORD,
    God of our father Israel,
    from everlasting to everlasting.
Yours, O LORD, is the greatness and the power
    and the glory and the majesty and the splendor,
    for everything in heaven and earth is yours.
Yours, O LORD, is the kingdom;
    you are exalted as head over all.
Wealth and honor come from you;
    you are the ruler of all things.
In your hands are strength and power
    to exalt and give strength to all.
Now, our God, we give you thanks,
    and praise your glorious name.

But who am I, and who are my people, that we should be able to give as generously as this? Everything comes from you, and we have given you only what comes from your hand."

David acknowledged the sovereignty of God over everything he had. If you and I are going to achieve financial freedom in our personal life, our family, our business, and in our church, then we're going to have to do the same. We're going to have to change our attitude toward money.

LIES THAT SOUND LIKE THE TRUTH

I'm going to share with you several lies that sound like the truth. When you read them you're going to say, "You know, they sound true"—but they're not.

Lie #1: All the church talks about is money.

Remember, don't be misled. It's a lie. The church doesn't talk *enough* about money and how to manage it. Consequently Christians are among some of the worst money managers in the world, even though they ought to be the best.

I have a number of banker friends. They tell me the worst risk for a bank is usually a church. That's why they don't like to extend loans to churches. The reason they don't want to is because churches are notorious for not paying off their loans and often end up going into receivership. No lending institution in its right mind wants to have the public relations' nightmare of having to foreclose on a church.

If that weren't bad enough, you know after the church who's the #2 risk to banks? Tragically, it's the pastor of the church. In far too many cases he's one of the worst financial managers there are. I always get nervous when I'm around pastors who want to know if there are discounts for them. (I've never asked for a discount in my life.) I've always said, "You pay me a salary and I'll do like everybody else. I don't need discounts." When somebody offers me a discount, I always say, "No thank you. I'll pay the regular price, whatever it is."

Christians, especially pastors, ought to be leading the world in the management of money, but we aren't. Why? I believe Lie #1, all the church talks about is money, trips more people up than we know. Here's how it works: The devil convinces you that all the church talks about is money. So whenever the issue of money comes up, you're already offended. Whether it's a small group, or you're out with Christian friends and the subject of money comes up, if the devil's convinced you that all the church talks about is money, you're already set to be offended.

Why does he do that? SO YOU AND I WON'T LISTEN TO GOD'S TRUTH. If the devil can get you upset or fired up, you won't listen up, and you'll miss the truth that can set you free! (Some of you are upset right now. Be honest. Aren't you? You're nervously squirming as you read this. Take three deep breaths and calm down.)

The devil sets us up so we won't listen to what God wants us to know. And as long as we don't know what God wants us to know, we can't possibly do what God wants us to do, and the result? The devil is able to keep us in bondage.

What do we need to do to avoid that? We need to change our attitude right in the face of the devil. We need to say, "My church needs to talk more about money and help people like me solve our financial problems and get out of debt!"

Lie #2: Money and things can satisfy me.

It sure sounds like the truth, doesn't it? But it's a lie. Money and things can't satisfy you. Money and things can satisfy for a while, but that's it.

Some of you will read this whole chapter and when you get in your car to go to work tomorrow you'll still believe this lie. I could write a hundred chapters on it, preach a hundred sermons on it, and some of you would still walk out the front door of your house tonight or tomorrow morning and say, "Well, I know what he says, but if I had that new car, I'd be pretty happy." "If I had that big house up on the hill overlooking the lake, I'd be pretty happy."

That's my point. We just don't believe it. But you need to know, IT'S A LIE! Every day we're bombarded with advertisements from Madison Avenue and Hollywood about things we need to get or have to have because they'll satisfy us. Oh, really? Ecclesiastes 5:10 says, "Whoever loves money never has money enough; whoever loves wealth is never satisfied with his income. This, too, is meaningless. As goods increase, so do those who consume them. And what benefit are they to the owner except to feast his eyes on them?"

You and I need to change our attitude. Money and things will never satisfy us. Only God can do that. That new car, that new house, that new suit, that new job, that new promotion, it's not going to satisfy you. Only God can do that.

Lie #3: *It's my money and I can do whatever I want with it.*

When I say this one, especially out loud, it really sounds like the truth. But it's a lie. The truth is, it's all God's money and you and I are simply managers of it. Psalm 24:1 says, "The earth is the LORD's and everything in it, the world, and all who live in it."

Let me share with you a parable Jesus told. Luke 12:16,

And he told them this parable: "The ground of a certain rich man produced a good crop. He thought to himself, 'What shall I do? I have no place to store my crops.'

"Then he said, 'This is what I'll do. I will tear down my barns and build bigger ones, and there I will store all my grain and my goods. And I'll say to myself, [notice how many times he says, "I, I'll, my, myself,"] "You have plenty of good things laid up for many years. Take life easy; eat, drink and be merry."'

"But God said to him, 'You fool! This very night your life will be demanded from you. Then who will get what you have prepared for yourself?'"

Now don't read into this what the devil wants you to read into it. The devil wants you to hear that when you get a certain amount of things in your life, God's going to yank you home to heaven. That's not what this is talking about. God's not against your having things. What Jesus is saying here is that this guy didn't have a clue. He thought he had all these wonderful possessions and could just sit back and enjoy them for a long time.

The reality is, when we die, all that stuff goes to somebody who didn't work for it anyway. I don't want to frighten you, but one of these days all the possessions you have and all the money you've got in the bank is going to belong to somebody else; and, in most cases, it will belong to somebody who didn't deserve it. You're going to leave it all behind. I'm going to leave it all behind. Job said, "Naked I came into this world, and naked I will go out of this world" (Job 1:21, paraphrase). We're going to leave it all behind. It's not ours. It all belongs to God.

So we need to change our attitude. We need to realize everything we have is on temporary loan from God, and it's our privilege to be a faithful manager of it for the time we're here on earth. It's just on temporary loan. Those clothes you're wearing, sir, are on loan from God. That nice car you're driving today, ma'am, is on loan from God. That beautiful home you have that God's blessed you with, you guessed it, is on loan from God for a little while. Be a faithful manager of it.

I've shared with you several lies that sound like the truth. Now let me give you some truths that sound like lies. Are you ready?

TRUTHS THAT SOUND LIKE LIES

Truth #1: God is the One Who determines how much money I have.

In Deuteronomy 8:17-18 Moses says, "You may say to yourself, 'My power and the strength of my hands have produced this wealth for me.' But remember the Lᴏʀᴅ your God, for it is he who gives you the ability to produce wealth, and so confirms his covenant, which he swore to your forefathers, as it is today." In other words what he's saying is, you can go out there and say, "I did this. My hands did this." The truth is, you had nothing to do with it. God's the One who gave you the ability to do it.

In Matthew 6:33 Jesus said, "But seek first God's kingdom and His righteousness, and then all these things will be added to you" (paraphrase). Jesus said, "Don't go after the things. The pagans run after all the stuff. You put God first and God will take care of everything else." Why? Because God is the One Who determines how much money we have; we don't. You and I need to change our attitude. God is the One Who determines my income, not me, not my company, not my hard work, not my brilliance, not my creativity. Therefore, I will put God first.

Truth #2: God has the power to shut down my company, my business, and dry up my source of income without a moment's notice.

Remember the story of Nebuchadnezzar in Daniel 3? He saw what happened to Shadrach, Meshach, and Abednego and said, "Their God has to be THE God. Everybody has to honor their God, and anybody who doesn't will be put to death" (paraphrase). Remember that? However, in Daniel 4:29 the Bible says, "Twelve months later [one year], as the king was walking on the roof of the royal palace of Babylon, he said, 'Is not this the great Babylon I have built as the royal residence, by my mighty power and for the glory of my majesty?'"

Nebuchadnezzar was walking around admiring his stuff. He was saying, "Wow, look at this. This is all mine. I did all this. Look what's been accomplished through my life and look at this business I've built. I've got all the bills paid and look at this stuff I've got. Things are going wonderful." And the Bible says,

The words were still on his lips when a voice came from heaven, "This is what is decreed for you, King Nebuchadnezzar: Your royal authority has been taken from you. You will be driven away from people and will live with the wild animals; you will eat grass like cattle. Seven times [or seven years] will pass by for you until you acknowledge that the Most High is sovereign over the kingdoms of men and gives them to anyone he wishes."

Immediately what had been said about Nebuchadnezzar was fulfilled. He was driven away from people and ate grass like cattle. His body was drenched with the dew of heaven until his hair grew like the feathers of an eagle and his nails like the claws of a bird.

In the next verse Nebuchadnezzar takes the pen and says, "I'd like to share my testimony. At the end of that time, I, Nebuchadnezzar, raised my eyes toward heaven, and my sanity was restored." I wish I could park there for about a half hour. Get your eyes on God and your sanity will be restored. (There's a sermon there.)

Nebuchadnezzar said,

Then I praised the Most High; I honored and glorified him who lives forever.

His dominion is an eternal dominion;
   his kingdom endures from generation to generation.
All the peoples of the earth
   are regarded as nothing.
He does as he pleases
   with the powers of heaven
   and the peoples of the earth.
No one can hold back his hand
   or say to him: "What have you done?"

At the same time that my sanity was restored, my honor and splendor were returned to me for the glory of my kingdom. My advisers and nobles sought me out, and I was restored to my throne and became even greater than before. Now I, Nebuchadnezzar, praise and exalt and glorify the King of heaven, because everything he does is right and all his ways are just. And those who walk in pride he is able to humble.

God has the power to shut down my company, my business, and yes, even my church and dry up my source of income on a moment's notice. So you and I need to change our attitude. We need to say, "I don't need to worry about the economy or the stock market. Instead I need to focus on living my life in a manner that honors and pleases God." What happens on Monday morning when Wall Street opens is not nearly as important as what happens on Sunday morning when God's Word is opened. We are acknowledging that God is the One Who can lift us up or shut us down. Any time He wants. We're not in control, God is. He's sovereignly in control of all things and all of us.

Truth #3: Giving to God is the only way out of my financial problems.

Sounds like a lie, doesn't it? Giving to God is the only way out of my financial problems. (I know what you're thinking.) But Jesus said, "Give, and it will be given to you."

I've been in full-time ministry since 1977, and in all those years I've watched people get into financial difficulty and financial problems, and the first place they cut back is in their giving to God. You can mark it down, sign it, seal it, and take it to the bank; when people get mad at the preacher or get mad at the church, the first thing they do is stop giving to God. You want to say to those people, "It's all right to get mad at me, but don't cut yourself off from the blessings of God."

There will be times when you disagree with your pastor (I know that's hard to believe) or you might get angry with something that happens in the church. But don't stop obeying God just because you're mad at somebody or some thing. You're just going to compound your problems and exacerbate your frustrations.

Someone will say, "Well, preacher, surely you aren't telling me, with the problems I've got and the debt I've got, that I ought to be giving back to God? God wouldn't want me to give, would He?" I've heard well-meaning preachers say, "Oh, no, God understands. God wouldn't want you to give." God doesn't say that. The people who are in financial difficulty are the very people who need to give. Why? I'll let Jesus answer it. "Give, and it will be given to you" (Luke 6:38).

I'm told there's an old shack out in the Arizona desert. Inside this shack is a water well, a pump, a jar of water, and a note. The note says: "If you use this water to prime the pump, you will have all the water you want to drink. If you drink the water in this jar, throw away this note." I don't think I need to expound upon that. The Apostle Paul said in 2 Corinthians 9:6, "Remember this: Whoever sows sparingly will also reap sparingly, and whoever sows generously will also reap generously." God is the One Who owns it all and distributes it all. It's not your business or your company. It's not your abilities or work ethic. It's not your brilliance or your charisma. It's God. It all begins with God. It all ends with God. And until we get that right, nothing else will work. Nothing.

You and I need to change our attitude. We need to say, "I'm willing to trust God and begin giving faithfully, systematically, and generously each week, so God can bless me out of my financial problems." And He will.

WHAT'S THE BEST WAY TO FINANCIAL FREEDOM?

You won't spend your way to financial freedom.

I've watched people get in financial difficulty, and they'll buy a new car. Now how in the world do they do that? If you're already in financial difficulty, how does that work? Or they'll buy new clothes. Or they'll go on some vacation. They'll say, "I just need to get away from it all." However, when you come back, it will all be waiting on you. It will all be there. And if you spent a lot of money, charging your vacation on little credit cards, there will be some big bills waiting for you when you get back. You won't spend your way to financial freedom.

You won't borrow your way to financial freedom.

"Well, all we need is a banker who has a great heart and he'll give us a debt consolidation loan." Not long ago I talked to a friend of mine who used to serve as president of one of the banks in our city about debt consolidation loans. I wanted to reconfirm that I was giving the right advice to people because I never encourage people to get debt consolidation loans. To me, that's the absolute last straw. Why? Because unless you deal with the problem at the faucet, unless you turn it off first, it doesn't matter what kind of nice hose you have or what kind of attachments you have. If you don't stop the flow you still have tremendous pressure building up, and sooner or later you'll be dealing with a flood.

So I asked my banker friend, "Does your bank do that?" He answered, "Yes, we do, but I'd want to sit down with those people and make sure they realize that's really not the source of the problem. That's the symptom."

The source of the problem is overspending. Living beyond your means. We've got to deal with that first. You won't borrow your way to financial freedom.

You won't cheat your way to financial freedom.

Someone will say, "What I'll do is adjust my taxes and keep some of the money the government is taking." Listen, if you do that, you're rebelling against Romans 13 where God says you need to obey the laws of the land. God up in heaven, Who determines your income and distributes wealth to you, is not going to honor the fact you're down here on earth cheating the IRS or anyone else.

You won't steal your way to financial freedom.

Someone says, "I know what I can do, I'll start adding a little bit of money to my expense reports each week. That way I'll get some extra money." No you won't. You're not going to steal your way to financial freedom.

You won't beg your way to financial freedom.

Have you noticed people holding cardboard signs that say, "Will work for food?" They are lying and they know it. Sorry. I know you're probably thinking, "This guy doesn't have an ounce of compassion." No, I'm just telling you the truth. Check the newspaper from your city and you'll find all kinds of places looking for people to work. Right here in our own area *The Fort Worth Star-Telegram* has between six and ten pages of Want Ads offering jobs. Or you can get a copy of *The Dallas Morning News* and you'll find twice that many ads wanting to give people jobs.

After conducting a wedding several years ago, I did a little experiment. I went in all the restaurants close to our church— McDonald's, Burger King, Taco Bueno, and Denny's—and I asked, "Do you have any jobs available?" They looked at me kind of funny because I was dressed in a black suit and tie and they said, "Well, yes." And I said, "No, no, no, not for me. I just wanted to know if you had any jobs available." Every one of them had jobs available.

Here's my point: In the time it takes to buy a magic marker and find a piece of cardboard for a sign, those people could've walked into McDonald's or someplace like it and said, "Could I work here?" and they'd gladly give them a job with benefits. They'll even give them a uniform to wear.

You're not going to beg your way to financial freedom. Someone says, "I'll just have my relatives pay." Listen, it's not your relatives' responsibility to take care of the fact you're a poor planner and a poor manager. I want to tell you something else.

It's not the church's responsibility either. Some people believe the church ought to be this big, wonderful bucket of free money, and whenever people overextend themselves or manage their money poorly, they erroneously believe the church ought to somehow give it away to anybody and everybody. (That's a subject for another book.)

You'd be shocked if you really studied what the Bible says about biblical benevolence. Did you know the Bible says if a person won't work, they're not supposed to eat? (Read 2 Thessalonians 3:10.) Did you know the Bible says the first people, the first support group that's supposed to take care of needy individuals is their own family members? (Read 1 Timothy 5:4-16.)

Be very careful when you start talking about benevolence and want to lay that burden on the doorstep of the church. The first group that's supposed to support you is your immediate and extended family. And if they don't do it, the Bible says they're worse than unbelievers.

You won't gamble your way to financial freedom.

Someone says, "What I'm going to do is buy a lottery ticket." I like to have fun with people who buy lottery tickets. When I get gas at the gas station, they're always in there. The lottery-lovers. It never fails. No matter what time of day I get gas, there's somebody buying lottery tickets, and I always say the same thing to them. "You know what? You might as well just take your money and throw it in that trash can over there." They give me the weirdest looks.

Someone says, "But, Preacher, if I won the lottery, I'd give that money to the church." We won't accept it. We will not accept money you got gambling. God in heaven wouldn't honor it. You say, "I'm going to win the lottery and I'm going to give all that money to the poor." Friend, that's who they're taking the money from in the first place! Statistics have proven the majority of people who purchase lottery tickets are those who can least afford it. God's not going to honor that. God won't bless that.

Someone else says, "I'm going to take this money and I'm going to Las Vegas." Now read this real slowly. You're going to take God's money. You're going to the devil's playground, and you're going to gamble it and make money for God and His kingdom? God's not going to honor that.

I've told people for years one of the reasons I don't buy lottery tickets is God would let me win. He would. I'd be the guy, if I went and bought a ticket, to win. You'd see it on the news. The reporter would say, "One ticket matched all 6 numbers or 7 numbers and it was purchased in Texas." And people in our church would say, "I wonder if it's somebody we know?" Then *The Star-Telegram* or *Dallas Morning News* would have my picture on the front page the next morning, and it would say, "Pastor Barry Cameron won all this money." And you know what? The elders would say, "Hit the street." My credibility would be crushed. That's one reason I don't buy lottery tickets. Joseph said, "How could I do such a thing like this and disgrace my God." Wouldn't it be wonderful if Christians would start standing up for principle and truth and say, "I can't gamble, I need to honor and trust God. God's the One Who takes care of me, not the lottery and not the one-armed bandits in Las Vegas."

GENUINE SHARING

Several years ago at a conference I heard John Maxwell tell the story of a congressman who took his son to McDonald's. The father bought his son a Coke and a large order of fries and they went and sat down. The father took a drink of his Coke and reached over to get a fry from his son, and his son put his hands around the fries and pulled them back. The father said, "That's okay, son." But as he sat there he started thinking to himself, "Doesn't my son realize I'm the one who gave him those fries in the first place? Doesn't he realize I can take those fries away from him any time I want? Doesn't he realize I can go up to the counter and buy all the fries I want? I can tell the people at the counter, 'Go out there and bury my son in French fries.' Doesn't my son realize I don't need any of his fries? I can get my own. Doesn't he realize all I wanted to do was share a couple of fries with him?" And then the congressman said it hit him. His son was simply acting like he'd been acting with God.

Do you see any parallel? God blesses us and says, "I want to sit down with you and enjoy some of those blessings." So God sits down, and when He starts to come to us, we put our hands around all our stuff and say, "No, no, no, this is ours, God. We'll decide what we are going to give you." And God in Heaven says, "Don't they realize I'm the source of everything they've got? Don't they realize I have the power to take whatever blessings I've given them? Don't they realize I can bury them in blessings if I want to? Don't they realize I don't need anything they have? I just wanted to share it with them."

Don't make the mistake of thinking you can achieve financial freedom on your own and ignore the sovereignty of God. Those are His fries.

Read Proverbs 1:20-23. Wisdom is speaking and wisdom says, "I called out in the streets and no one would listen. Therefore, I will laugh at them when calamity comes" (paraphrase). Who is wisdom? Wisdom is literally God. God is saying, "I lay it out there. I tell My people here's what I want you to do, but if they won't listen, what else can I do? They come running when they're in a mess, but what can I do? I tried to prevent it from ever happening by giving them the very principles that could've ensured their prosperity."

You're going to read about some phenomenal principles in this book. But if you don't apply them to your life, they won't do you any good. God wants to bless us, and He wants to prosper us, but we're the ones who decide whether it's going to happen or not.

The first step on the road to financial freedom is to change our attitude and acknowledge the sovereignty of God in our finances. "God, I want Your way. I want Your wisdom. I want Your guidance. I want to follow Your principles, and I want Your blessings in my life."

If you will make that commitment, you're already on your way to getting out of financial bondage and well on your way to financial freedom.

FROM THE
GOOD FILE
Simple ideas to encourage you to
GET OUT OF DEBT

Getting into debt is easy. Getting out isn't. That's why it takes so much time, effort, and commitment. But if you'll invest in your future by doing what you ought to do now to get out of debt, you'll enjoy a multitude of dividends and benefits in the days ahead.

Trust in God, self-denial, and discipline are three major keys! We have to develop a nonnegotiable strategy when it comes to our finances. Just like the training regimen for an Olympic athlete that has to begin years before the actual event, we, too, have to discipline ourselves to do what we ought to do now if we want to be out of debt later.

But here's where the trouble begins. Some people are willing to pray and ask God for help, but that's where it ends. They want God to do it all and are unwilling to do anything themselves. Others start out great but get discouraged and give up. "It's too hard," they say.

Still others are unwilling to give up anything or deny themselves something now so they can enjoy everything later. "I'm going to enjoy life now," they say, little knowing that the more they enjoy (indulge) themselves now, the harder it will be to enjoy themselves in the future. The saying, "Play now and pay later, or pay now and play later," is certainly true when it comes to the stewardship of our finances.

Proverbs 24:27 says, "Finish your outdoor work and get your fields ready; after that, build your house." Translation: do what you ought to do first, then you can do what you want to do.

Action Plans
Getting out of debt will require us to:

A. **Trust in God**—He is the One Who gives you the ability to produce wealth. Start trusting Him alone for your finances.

B. Practice self-denial—Until you learn to control impulse spending and binge buying, you won't be able to get out of debt.

C. Be self-disciplined—No one is going to do it for you. Learn to say no, and go without those things you are tempted to buy.

If we'll do these three things on a consistent basis, over an extended period of time and not give up, the day will come when we can say, "I'm free forever from the bondage of debt!"

CHAPTER 2

BONDAGE

"Debt keeps you stuck in the trap of using your future to pay for your past."
—Mary Hunt

Let's review for a moment.

- We've already seen that the devil tries to deceive us into believing that all the church talks about is money.
- We learned that the devil tries to get us to believe money and things can satisfy us.
- We learned that the devil tries to convince us it's our money and we can do whatever we want with it.
- We learned that God is the One Who determines how much money we have.
- We learned that giving to God is the only way out of our financial problems.
- Whenever you see or hear the word INTEREST, I want you to immediately think of two words: SOMEBODY ELSE. Because anytime you're paying interest, SOMEBODY ELSE is making money instead of you.
- Remember the French fry illustration with the congressman and his son? Don't ever forget, the French fries belong to God.

So the first step on the road to our financial freedom is to acknowledge the sovereignty of God, not only in our finances, but also in every area of our lives. Now we're ready to move to step two.

The second step on the road to financial freedom is: **We need to be aware of and avoid the subtlety of debt.**

THE BONDAGE OF DEBT

A few years ago in the course of one week I received five envelopes in the mail from credit card companies offering me new credit cards. One offered me, because of my "good credit standing," up to $50,000 on their card at 2.9% interest for the first nine months. One card said, because of my good credit standing, they'd give me $100,000 to spend. (On a credit card!) I told Mel Dietz, our Executive Pastor, "I could buy a car or a home with this."

Not one of these five credit card company applications mentioned the word debt anywhere. In fact, some of those credit card applications said I could take balances from other credit cards and put it on theirs for an incredibly low 2.9% rate and everything would be fine.

I kept reading and when I got way down to the itsy-bitsy, teeny-weeny, fine print, it said as long as I participated in their credit plan, things would be fine. But at the end of nine months the rate jumped to 16% on one, 22% on another. Honestly, that's the most ridiculous loan I could ever take out in my entire life.

Our local paper ran a full-page ad for a leading furniture company. I asked my wife, "What sticks out to you in this ad?" It said, "12 Months, No Interest." I saw the word interest, and what are the first two words that came to my mind? You're right: SOMEBODY ELSE! I read the ad and it said as long as you keep making the payments according to the company's revolving credit plan everything was fine.

WHAT CREDIT CARD COMPANIES DON'T WANT YOU TO KNOW

Don't miss this. Remember the word "revolving." The credit card companies call good-credit people, in other words, people who use their credit cards regularly and only pay the monthly payment required, "revolvers." (Sounds like something that, when loaded, can be dangerous, doesn't it? Just a thought.)

Credit card companies want you, me, and everybody in the world to be a "revolver." If they can get us to be "revolvers," people who will just keep making the minimum payment each month and keep revolving that debt over and over again, they can make a lot of money off us. They love "revolvers."

Guess what they call people like me who pay their credit cards off and never keep a balance that rolls over to the next month? This is the absolute truth. They call people like me "deadbeats." If you pay your credit card off each month, the credit card industry considers you a deadbeat! I'd call you a genius, but we'll get into that later.

So I read the whole ad, saw this beautiful furniture, and read this "12 Months, No Interest" offer. I went to the bottom of the ad to the ultrasmall, fine print, and it said, "at any point if you fail to make your minimum monthly payment, the interest rate goes to 21%." Just like that. Again, the ad didn't mention debt anywhere on the page.

Debt is subtle and those who try to encourage us to get into debt are subtle themselves and sometimes even sinister as well. That's why we need to always read the fine print before we foolishly pursue debt of any amount.

GOD'S WILL IS FOR US TO BE DEBT FREE

In Deuteronomy 28 we find some incredibly sound financial advice. I'll tell you right up front that I believe without a shadow of a doubt it's God's will for us to be debt free.

Look at these verses beginning in Deuteronomy 28:12: "The LORD will open the heavens, the storehouse of his bounty, to send rain on your land in season and to bless all the work of your hands. You will lend to many nations but will borrow from none." God doesn't say borrowing is wrong. Don't read that into the verse; nowhere does it say borrowing is wrong. But He says, "You're going to live in such a way (God's people) that you'll lend to other nations and you'll borrow from no one." That's His plan. The next verse says, "The LORD will make you the head and not the tail. If you pay attention to the commands of the LORD your God that I give you this day and carefully follow them, you will always be at the top, never at the bottom. Do not turn aside from any of the commands I give you today, to the right or to the left, following other gods and serving them."

It's very clear. God does not want us to be in debt. He wants us to be "lenders" instead of "borrowers." Unfortunately the majority of people in the Christian community are seriously and severely in debt.

"Lenders and not borrowers" doesn't describe the average church in America. It doesn't describe the average Christian either. Yet God said, "I want you to be free so you can lend to many and borrow from none." Do I have your attention?

I received an e-mail in December of 1999 from one of our church members. I asked permission to share it. It said,

> I for one am looking forward to your January series on being debt free. Paul and I have been totally debt free since February 25, 1997. That was when we made the last payment on our house. We had a 30-year loan, paid it off in 7 years, and it is a great feeling. We feel the Lord has been very good to us. I still like hearing things on finances and debt because I still learn things.[1]

I received another e-mail the same week from another family in our church and asked permission to share theirs.

I wanted to thank you for your powerful message today. My wife and I have been visiting the church for awhile now and are signed up for the Membership Class on the 9th. Your message on getting out of debt became a reality to us about eight years ago. We both fell under conviction about this and resolved to become totally debt free. Well, we have as of several years ago now. I can only attempt to say one does not fully understand the yoke one is under until they are free. We will never go back to that bondage.[2]

That's exactly what I want to deal with in this chapter: The bondage of debt. If I do my job correctly in these next few pages, you will never again be able to look at the word "debt" or hear the word "debt" and not get a sick feeling in your stomach. I want to teach you to hate debt. I want to help you get to the place where, when you see the word, or hear somebody talking about it that you'll just say to yourself (and perhaps them as well), "I hate debt." Because one of the most important factors on the road to financial freedom is having a proper understanding of the bondage of debt.

Have you ever stopped to consider what it would be like to be completely out of debt? Have you ever imagined what life would be like if you didn't owe anything to anyone? Have you ever dreamed about that? Have you ever thought, "If this coming Friday I could get my paycheck and it wasn't pre-obligated to anyone and I could do anything I wanted with it, what would life be like?" (Made you feel good, didn't I?)

Just the thought of being out of debt gives you a great feeling. Why? Because you weren't created to live in bondage.

Listen carefully because I want to explain something. Your entire life would be absolutely different than what it is right now if you were out of debt. We all know it would sure be nice to get there. But some aren't willing to make the decisions and develop the disciplines it takes to get there. Like an Olympic athlete who wants to participate in the Olympics but spends every morning of his life at the donut shop. Sorry, it's not going to happen. It's not going to work out. You might have a great dream. But if you're nibbling on chocolate-covered, cream-filled donuts every morning, the chances of your even attending the Olympics are slim.

Just think of the possibilities if you were totally and completely debt free. Think for a moment what would happen at your church. Can you imagine what your church could do if everyone in your church were debt free? (Made you feel good again, didn't I?)

Think what your church could do if everyone in your church were totally and completely debt free. Can you imagine a missionary visiting and he shares with one of the ushers, "I'm on my way to Brazil. They routed our flight through here and it got delayed last night. So I can't fly out until this afternoon. I'd always heard about your church and wanted to come and worship with you. So I'm here today."

The usher says to the missionary, "What are you going to be doing in Brazil?" The missionary answers, "I'm going to try to be an encouragement to them, train some preachers, and help build a building." So the usher says, "What will you need to do all that?" And the missionary replies, "We're praying God will give us $100,000." So the usher says, "Go ahead and go on into the service and I'll get back with you."

The usher goes to the Executive Pastor and says, "We've got a visiting missionary with us today and he needs $100,000 to go to Brazil. Wouldn't it be great if we helped him?" The Executive Pastor checks with a few elders and gets the pastor and says, "We'd like for you to make a small announcement at the end of the service and see if we can help this missionary out."

Now follow me. As astounding as what I am about to tell you is going to appear, it's absolutely possible. If the people in your church were out of debt, you could give that fellow not only $100,000, you could probably receive an offering for $400,000.

Someone says, "Oh my goodness. What would we do with the extra $300,000?" Give it to the missionary. What a blessing that would be. And no one would have to sacrifice because you were debt free.

Regrettably the reality in most churches is that they probably can't do something like that this coming Sunday morning. You know why? Because the average church in America and the average church member in America is so miserably in debt, if they received an offering at the close of the regular Sunday service, it would more likely be $4,000 ... or less.

Tell me which scenario does a better job honoring God? We need to get out of debt. If you can't think of enough reasons in your own heart and life to want to get out of debt, let that be a motivation to you. To be a part of a church where there wouldn't be a single need that couldn't be met, including visiting missionaries who need $100,000.

I've been praying for years to be a part of a church that could give $1 million to missions in one calendar year. But you know what I'm praying now? I believe one of the reasons God burdened me to help get our church out of debt is so we can receive a $1 million offering for missions in one day. Yes, you read it right: in one day. Now we're not going to be able to do it next week, but I do believe we will get to the place where that will happen.

If every member of our church were out of debt, it wouldn't take any sacrifice to receive a one-day offering of a million dollars. But in most churches, if you started talking like that, people would start getting nervous because an offering of that magnitude for missions in one day is unheard of and would take considerable sacrifice. But it shouldn't make anyone nervous at all.

What I'm trying to get you to do is get a visual picture of how your life and your church are being seriously and drastically affected by debt. Miserable, worthless, ridiculous, life-killing, happiness-destroying debt. Do you get the picture yet?

I think you already know God doesn't want His church to be that way. In fact, Peter Wagner wrote a book called *Churchquake,* and in it he tells the story of two churches. These are his words: "These churches seem to have all the money they need to accomplish whatever they perceive God is calling them to do. They are both out of debt."[3] Listen to this: "Crenshaw Christian Center is an African-American church in the inner city of Los Angeles pastored by Fred Price. When they outgrew their building on Crenshaw Avenue, they purchased the old Pepperdine University Campus and built the Faith Dome, a worship center that has 10,146 theater seats. The total cost was $26 million: $14 million for the land, $12 million for the building."[4]

Dr. Wagner was invited to be their guest for the three-hour dedication service. And he said that the grand finale of their dedication service, the first service in the new building, was when Fred Price took a letter out of his pocket from the Security Pacific bank and it read, "Paid in full."

There's an outstanding book called *Debt-Free Living* by Larry Burkett. If you don't have it, you need to get it. Listen to what he wrote: "Regardless of how it seems today, debt is not normal in any economy and should not be normal for God's people. We live in a debt-ridden society that is now virtually dependent on a constant expansion of credit to keep the economy going. That is a symptom of a society no longer willing to follow God's directions."[5]

Years ago our Executive Pastor, Mel Dietz, and I were out looking for a small TV to give to one of the missionaries our church supports. We went around to several stores and finally bought one. By the way, we paid cash for it. (You've got to practice what you preach.)

When we were out driving around, Mel said, "You would've

thought it was Christmas at all these stores today." I agreed and added, "Look at all these vehicles. You know people are miserably in debt and there they go, walking into the store, to get even more miserably in debt. Then they'll walk into a church like ours on Sunday, and we'll say we've got a missionary from Brazil who has a need and they'll respond, "Oh, all that church wants is my money." We both laughed. But it really isn't funny when you think about it.

Isn't it sad how that works? The devil leads us into debt so he can keep us in bondage and keep us from doing great things for God and His kingdom.

DOES THE BIBLE FORBID GOING INTO DEBT?

No. But it sure discourages us from going into debt. Let me give you some Biblical principles. I'll share seven of them from the Bible.

Seven Biblical Principles about Debt

1. Going into debt makes you a servant to someone other than God. In Proverbs 22:7 Solomon says, "The rich rule over the poor, and the borrower is servant to the lender." When you borrow, instead of God being your Lord and God being your boss, somebody else is calling the shots. Let me warn you, when you're not able to make the payments, they'll start calling some shots you don't want to hear.

2. It's clearly a sin if you borrow and don't repay. That's very clear in the Bible. Psalm 37:21 says, "The wicked borrow and do not repay, but the righteous give generously." Whenever I see the Bible say, "the righteous give generously," the reason I believe they can give generously is, they're out of debt.

3. The Bible warns it's better not to go into debt. You're not going to believe this verse. Proverbs 17:18 says, "A man lacking in judgment strikes hands in pledge and puts up security for his neighbor." I read that in the NIV and thought it sounded weird. It sounds like you and me going into debt for our neighbors. So I did some checking on it and guess what the literal translation of the Hebrew is? It says, "The man lacking in judgment strikes hands in pledge, makes an agreement for debt in the presence of his neighbor." Makes a whole lot of difference, doesn't it? It's not the fact that I'm going into debt for my neighbor. That would almost seem as if I were being a Good Samaritan, doing something nice for my neighbor. But that's not what it's talking about. It's saying a man lacking in judgment, a foolish man, goes into debt, and his neighbor knows about it.

I can't wait for my neighbors to drive up and down our street. We might not have the nicest cars in the neighborhood or the nicest house, but they're all going to know our house and our cars are paid for. People drive by our church and look at our facilities and our grounds, and they may not understand all the different buildings and what they're used for, but wouldn't it be wonderful for them to know they're all paid for.

4. The longest term of debt God's people took on in the Bible was seven years. In Deuteronomy 15:1 God says, "At the end of every seven years you must cancel debts." Now I know some of you will read that and say, "That would be great. That would be wonderful." Keep reading. "This is how it is to be done: Every creditor shall cancel the loan he has made to his fellow Israelite." Now it's interesting, God doesn't say he should have never made the loan in the first place, but He says, "Now is the time you should cancel it."

The Bible doesn't forbid borrowing. The Bible doesn't forbid debt. It just says there's a whole lot better way to live without it. Keep reading.

He shall not require payment from his fellow Israelite or brother, because the LORD's time for canceling debts has been proclaimed. You may require payment from a foreigner, but you must cancel any debt your brother owes you. However, there should be no poor among you, for in the land the LORD your God is giving you to possess as your inheritance, he will richly bless you, if only you fully obey the LORD your God and are careful to follow all these commands I am giving you today. For the LORD your God will bless you as he has promised, and you will lend to many nations but will borrow from none. You will rule over many nations but none will rule over you.

5. When you're in debt you are not in control of your own future. James 4:13-15 says, "Now listen, you who say, 'Today or tomorrow we will go to this or that city, spend a year there, carry on business and make money.' Why, you do not even know what will happen tomorrow. What is your life? You are a mist that appears for a little while and then vanishes." You don't know that you're going to have more money down the road to pay for what you're going into debt for. You can't possibly know that. But the salesman will tell you you can.

Several years ago I bought a Toyota Starlet. They don't even make them anymore. It wasn't much bigger than a bicycle. Honestly, it's the smallest car I've ever seen. (Like a go-cart with doors.) But it was all I could afford. The salesman's name, I'll never forget it, was Hank Williams. No, he didn't sing, but he gave me quite a song and told me, "This is a good starter car for you." What he didn't know was it wasn't a starter car for me. I'd already had six or seven. But I'd gotten so miserably in debt that it was all I could afford. He said, "You know, you'll come back here in a couple years so flush with cash. You're going to get that Toyota Supra right there. I can put you in that thing. Man, you're going to make so much money." Unfortunately what he said never happened. In fact, Toyota stopped making the Supra. But remember, he was a salesman. He was already talking me into the fact that I needed to come back and buy a bigger car because I was going to be making more money. We don't know that. We're not in control of our own future. We have no guarantees.

6. When you go into debt you are asking someone other than God to meet your needs. That's very dangerous. Paul said in Philippians 4:19, "And my God will meet all your needs according to his glorious riches in Christ Jesus." When we go into debt, we are trusting First National Bank or First Security or the Credit Union or whatever the name of your bank is instead of God.

7. When you go into debt and mortgage your future, you affect your whole family. In Proverbs 11:28-29 Solomon says, "Whoever trusts in his riches will fall, but the righteous will thrive like a green leaf. He who brings trouble on his family will inherit only wind, and the fool will be servant to the wise."

I think it's pretty clear in the Bible: Debt is not a good thing for us and does not represent God's perfect will for our lives.

DEFINITIONS FOR DEBT

Let me give you two terrific definitions for debt. This will help you have the right attitude toward debt. 1) Debt is a: Dumb Explanation for Buying Things. D-E-B-T. 2) If you have to use debt to buy something (D-E-B-T), think of these words: Don't Even Buy That.

Now remember, when you see the word "interest," I want you to think of two words: SOMEBODY ELSE, and when you think of debt, here's what I want you to think of: Been there, done with that. D-E-B-T is a dumb excuse for buying things. I'm not going to do it anymore.

There's a book out by Mary Hunt called *Debt-Proof Living*. Mary says, "For fun, I looked up the word debt in my trusty Thesaurus. Here's what it said: Debt—obligation, encumbrance, in the red, pound of flesh, arrears, inability to pay, bilked, bound, beholden, up to one's ears, over one's head, mortgaged to the hilt, in the poverty trap, unable to keep the wolf from the door, hard-up, beaten down, financially embarrassed, strapped, stripped, fleeced, busted."[6]

Are you getting the picture about debt yet? It's not good. In fact, Mary Hunt says there's only five things you can do with money:

1. You can give it. (That's the top of her list. Mine, too!)

2. You can save it.

3. You can invest it.

4. You can lend it.

5. You can spend it.[7]

There are only five things you can do with your money. So why blow it by getting in debt and losing it through paying interest to somebody else? It makes no sense whatsoever.

You may be sitting there reading this and saying, "I don't know if I can ever get out of debt." Can you get out of debt? Absolutely. Regardless of who you are. Regardless of how much debt you're in. I just hope you're not one of these people who walks around saying, "My dad was always in debt. My grandfather was always in debt." If I had the time, I'd debate that statement with you. Because when you go back to the time when people lived who are your grandfather's age and your great-grandfather's age, you'll quickly discover they didn't live lives of debt. They paid for things with cash. They were smarter than we are. Something else you may not know about those "good old days;" they didn't have to lock their doors at night, and they could leave the keys in their cars overnight. Now everything's changed, and not necessarily for the better. I believe anybody can get out of debt if they really want to and are willing to do what it takes to get out of debt.

According to the Theory of Aerodynamics as demonstrated

through wind tunnel tests, the bumblebee can't fly. Scientifically, aerodynamically, the bumblebee cannot fly. All the math, all the science says the bumblebee cannot fly because of its size, its weight, the shape of its body in relation to its total wing spread. Flying is scientifically impossible. But the bumblebee doesn't pay attention to science and math or the Theory of Aerodynamics. The bumblebee, being totally ignorant of scientific theory, flies anyway.

You can get out of debt, you just have to want to, and you have to be willing to do what it takes to get there.

HOW DO YOU GET OUT OF DEBT?

1. Make the irrevocable commitment to God and to yourself that you're going to get out of debt.

Make that commitment to God first, make it to yourself, and then share it with as many other people as you can so they can hold you accountable. If they see you pull in the driveway with a brand new car two weeks after you said you were going to get out of debt, they're going to say, "Uh, wait a minute." We need that kind of accountability to be successful.

2. Don't take on any more debt.

Just say, "That's it. I'm not borrowing anything else. I'm not going into debt." If you have to use debt to buy something, say to yourself, "Don't even buy that." It's a dumb explanation for buying things.

3. Put God first in your giving.

By the way, that doesn't mean you just throw God a bone every week, a little dollar or whatever change you've got in your pocket. The Bible teaches emphatically, as a minimum, that each of us should tithe the first 10% of our income back to God. Our first fruits belong to God. If we're not doing that, we'll never get out of debt.

4. Develop a written plan.

Some people don't like the word budget. For years, I did a lot of counseling, especially premarital counseling and marriage counseling. Every time I counseled people, they'd end up talking about financial problems, and I'd talk about budgets. Couples would say to me, "Oh yeah, it's a good thing to have a budget." And I'd always ask, "Do you have one?" In almost every case they'd answer, "Well, no, we're working on that."

Get a budget. My wife and I have a five-page budget. I can tell you from personal experience it's one of the secrets to getting out of debt and staying out of debt. Why? Because it helps you see where you are financially. One of the first things you need to do is get an accurate picture in print (in black and white) of what a mess you're in. That's where you need to start. It's not fun. It's not a full-blown party writing down all those bills and all those obligations, seeing you have a whole lot more going out than you have coming in. But you need to do that. That's where budgeting starts.

Our five-page budget shows how much our income is, what our bills are, what our obligations are, what's in savings, what's in retirement. On a weekly basis we know every dime we have and every responsibility we have. We have a list of which bills are coming next week and which ones need to be paid. It's incredibly helpful and informative, and it's not hard. It's not rocket science either. It's common sense.

You don't have to be a great mathematician to have a budget, but you need to have a written plan. You need to see what's really happening in your finances. By the way, as long as you have debt, you don't have true savings. You need to know that. It's good to have savings. I encourage you to do that. But just remember, as long as you have debt, you don't really have savings. Especially if you're earning interest of 4% on your savings and yet still paying off credit card debts with an interest rate of between 19-21%.

5. Set an attainable time frame to get out of debt.

Larry Burkett taught that anyone can be out of debt in seven years. But you may say, "I don't know; that might be too much pressure." Then put eight years down. But set a time. Set a goal. "We're going to be debt free by a specific day." If you don't set a goal, you'll never do it.

Several years ago there was a fellow sitting in my home; he was quite a bit overweight. We were both eating dessert, and he began telling me how he was going to lose weight. I thought, "Now isn't this funny. Here we are eating dessert, and you're talking about losing weight." But isn't that the way we are? We lay in bed and watch people working out on TV. We see those rock-hard abs and say, "Yeah, that's what I'm going to be like." Then we go downstairs and get a bowl of ice cream and a plate of cookies.

There has to be a goal or you're going to be in the same position or even worse by this time next year. You need to say, "I'm going to do this," and you're going to have to go without some things and make some changes in your lifestyle.

6. Adjust your lifestyle.

You don't have to go out to eat everyday. The worst investment you make on a daily basis is paying $1.75-$2.50 for iced tea or soda. It only costs them 10 to 20 cents. So they love it when you say, "Oh yes, I'll have a large root beer." Sure, no problem. As they walk away, they're saying, "Profit, profit, profit." Then they'll ask, "Would you like to start with an appetizer?" You know what an appetizer is for a restaurant? More money for them. You say, "Well, if I took a sack lunch to work, people would make fun of me." That's fine. Let them make fun of you until you're out of debt and then they'll come and ask, "How did you do that sack lunch deal? Can you teach me how to get out of debt?"

You don't have to go out to dinner every Friday night. You don't have to go out to movies. You don't have to stop and always get something at the store. Some people go to the mall on a weekly basis and can't walk out unless they have a bag in their hands. Let me give you a suggestion. Go to the mall today, walk the whole length of it, get in your car, and go home with nothing in your hand. Trust me. It will make you feel good. You can say, "I did it, I did it. I walked around the mall and didn't have to buy anything."

I love books. But I learned a long time ago, sometimes it's good for me to walk into a bookstore pick up a bunch of books, handle them, put them down, and walk out just to prove I'm still in control. That bookstore doesn't own me.

You'll never get out of debt if you don't adjust your lifestyle. There will always be people who make fun of you. There will always be people who don't understand you. And that's all right. When our family first made the decision to get out of debt, my son came to me and said, "Dad, you know there's some people making fun of you?" I said, "Yeah. So what?" He said, "Dad, I still think you're doing what's right." I said, "Son, I know I am. One of these days we're going to be debt free, and they won't be making fun of us anymore."

You can't let the critics and the people who make fun of you rule your life. That's one of the reasons so many are in debt and such a mess now. We listen to other people who said this is a good deal, try this, get that, buy this. We don't have to have what they have or buy what they tell us to buy. We need to get out of debt and then it won't matter what they say. In fact, they'll probably come to you and ask if you'd be willing to help them get out of debt.

Here's what our family did to get out of debt:
- We all went on strict budgets and there were no exceptions.
- We cancelled our subscription to the local newspaper and to USA TODAY.

- We cancelled all magazine subscriptions.
- We cancelled cable TV.
- We took sack lunches to school and work (all of us).
- We didn't go out to eat.
- We stopped getting our dog groomed.
- We didn't go to movies.
- We cut back on haircuts.
- We didn't go to concerts.
- We didn't do any special treatments for my wife or our girls like nails, perms, etc.
- We didn't go to sporting events.
- We didn't go anywhere you had to purchase a ticket.
- We had our older kids get jobs.
- We started drinking water instead of paying for coffee, tea or soft drinks.
- We turned down a lot of invitations to do things in order to save money.
- We went without new clothes for two years.
- We didn't go on any vacations or trips for two years.
- We carpooled to church to save on gas.
- We had a garage sale.
- We turned the thermostat up in the summer and down in the winter.
- We turned lights off when we left a room.
- We unplugged anything that blinked, buzzed, hummed, or gave any indication it was costing us money unless we were using it.
- We consolidated all trips to conserve gas.
- We stopped watering our grass. (Yes, our yard turned to dirt.)
- We didn't leave the water running while we brushed our teeth.
- We took less baths and shorter showers.
- We used coupons when shopping for groceries and necessities.

- We used birthday money, Christmas money, etc., to pay down the mortgage on our house.
- We reduced what we normally spent on Christmas and only gave gifts to each other that were practical – things we needed.
- We informed extended family members we wouldn't be exchanging gifts in order to help us get out of debt.
- We didn't put Christmas lights on the outside of our house.
- We didn't buy furniture.
- We didn't buy DVDs or CDs.
- We had our kids pay for their own stuff at school, camp, etc.
- We developed a laser focus of paying off our debts, including our mortgage, and looked for every dime and dollar we could find to do so.
- We used less of everything: shampoo, tooth paste, etc., so it would last longer.

7. Begin to systematically pay off all your debts.

You need to have a *written* plan. You need to look at your obligations and then start paying them off. I recommend you pay the smallest ones off first. Then use the money that used to go for those to pay for the next one.

Some people say, "You need to pay off the highest interest rate first." If you do the math, you'll figure out it doesn't work any better than if you just pay off the smallest one first. Start with the smallest one and, I assure you, if you've got a written plan, and you're able to cross one off, "That debt's gone," it will give you encouragement and momentum to get after the other obligations and eventually enable you to get out of debt.

Someone wrote these words called "It Can't Be Done."

> The ones who miss all the fun
>   are those who say it can't be done.
> In solemn pride they stand aloof
>   and greet each venture with reproof.

> Had they the power to face
>> the history of the human race.
> We'd have no radio or motor cars,
>> no streets lit by electric stars.
> No telegraph or telephone.
>> We'd linger in the age of stone.
> The world would sleep if things were run
>> by those who say, "It can't be done."

It can be done. And I want to encourage you: I'm committed to raising up an army of people who are absolutely, completely, and permanently debt free. I'm absolutely committed to it. You can do it. *Everyone* can do it.

Not only can it be done, it will be done. With God's help and for God's glory we can all be debt free. As I said earlier in this chapter, I believe there's no question God wants us out of debt. I also believe there's no question God is willing to do whatever it takes to get us out of debt. How do I know that? You and I entered this world in debt to sin. God knew that wasn't good. So He sent His own Son to pay off the debt we could never pay in order that we could be free. John 8:36 says, "So if the Son sets you free, you will be free indeed." There's no freedom and certainly no feeling in the world like being free from the debt of sin. The next best feeling is to be free from the debts of this world. God will help you with those, too!

FROM THE

GOOD FILE

Simple ideas to encourage you to
GET OUT OF DEBT

Three Essentials to Getting Out of Debt

1. What you SAY. If you continually say, "We'll never get out of debt," GUESS WHAT? You won't. The Bible says, "As a man thinks in his heart, so is he." You've got to change your conversation. Start thanking God for helping you get out of debt and continually tell your spouse, your family, and your friends, "Not only can we do it (get out of debt), we're going to do it." And watch what happens.

2. What you SPEND. If you continually overspend your income, you'll never get out of debt. You have to change your spending habits. Here are some ideas of things you can control: going out to eat, magazine and newspaper subscriptions, long distance phone calls, electricity, cell phone calls, buying new clothes, etc. Your debts and the interest you have to pay on them will continue to control your life and your future until you get your spending under control.

3. What you SAVE. Resist the urge to splurge. Don't spend everything you earn. Try to make it through every week with something left over you can save, even if it's only $5. You don't have to see the newest movie that just came out. You don't have to have the latest CD or DVD. Postpone those types of pleasures and put the money in savings. You'll quickly realize the folly of impulse purchases and the security that comes from having a nest egg of any size drawing interest for you.

Take some GOOD advice, watch what you SAY, what you SPEND, and what you SAVE. It'll help you get out of debt!

Action Plans

    A. Post your commitment to get out of debt in a visible place. It will keep you motivated daily.

    B. Cut one of your frivolous expenses from your budget. Replace it with a free equivalent.

    C. If your employer will do this, see if you can get part of your paycheck automatically deposited in a savings account every month. It's one way to force yourself to save.

CHAPTER 3

CHOICE

---

*"When we eat out, most of us expect to tip
the waiter or waitress 15 percent.
When we suggest 10 percent as a minimum church offering,
some folks are aghast."*
—Felix A. Lorenz, Jr.

Many people try to laugh away their financial problems or smile and act like everything's okay. Truth is, there's nothing funny about having financial problems. Having had more than my fair share of them, I think I can say with some degree of authority there's nothing funny about financial problems or financial stress. So why put on a charade for others and act like nothing's wrong?

Someone wisely said, "Too often we spend money we don't have for things we don't need to impress people we don't even know." Someone else said, "When our outgo exceeds our income, then our upkeep will become our downfall." There's nothing fun or funny about living with financial pressure and stress. There's nothing inherently humorous or enjoyable about living with bills, burdens, and the bondage of debt. Yet the majority of people live under the bondage of continual financial problems, financial stress, and miserable debt. It's a sad commentary on our society.

WHO'S BEHIND YOUR FINANCIAL PROBLEMS?

Before we can solve our financial problems, we need to find out who's behind them. Who's responsible for the financial mess we're in? When you get the answer, you're going to be shocked. Once we know who's behind our financial problems, then we're going to discover how we can solve them. Now make no mistake about it; you have a very significant role in your own financial problems through the choices you make. But there's somebody else behind your financial problems, and it's not your wife, your husband, or any other family member or friend.

If you study the Scriptures, it's very clear the devil wants you and me to be up to our ears in financial problems. He wants us to be up to our eyeballs in financial trouble, but even he's not the one responsible for our financial problems.

The shocking reality is, God is the One Who's behind our financial problems. Yes, you read it right. Almighty God! Here's the irony of it all: you and I can get out of our financial problems anytime we want. Literally, we can get out of our financial difficulties and get out from under the stress of our financial problems any time we want to. But we have to choose to do it *God's way.*

Personal Choice

Some will be shocked to read this statement, but no one is predestined to live his or her life in financial trouble. Ever known people who always seem to have cars that break down? Ever known people who always seem to have a major crisis going on at their house? Last week it was the dishwasher that blew up. Last month it was the washer that went bad. The month before that one of their kids was in a car wreck They just seem to have one financial calamity after another. It's so easy for us to look at them and say, "Well, they're just one of those people predestined to have financial problems their whole life." Where did you hear that? The Bible doesn't teach that anyone is predestined to be in financial trouble their entire life. We have the power to choose. You and I can choose to have a life that is drastically different from the life others choose.

Years ago when my son was still in high school, I took him to a Doc Severinsen concert in Fort Worth. Yes, he found the money in his budget to go, paid for his own ticket, and even bought our dinner. As we walked out of Wendy's (I know it's not the best restaurant in Fort Worth), I said, "Thanks, son, for dinner." (That's got a nice ring to it, don't you think?) We went to the concert and the average age of the people had to be sixty years and older. They were all dressed in coats and ties and nice dresses. We weren't dressed up quite that nice. We were sitting in the upper box level and as we looked around I said, "Matt, are any of your friends here, any of the other guys you know who play trumpet?" He said, "No, they're not here." And I said, "Well, it's great that you come to concerts like this because when you're exposed to things like this, it raises your sights and your vision for what you can do." (My son was and is quite a trumpet player.)

As we sat there, I tried to encourage him. I told him, "If you'll always do what others don't, you'll always get what other's won't." And that's true for finances. If you'll make the right choices in your life and do what other people are not willing to do, if you'll be willing to follow God and trust Him when it comes to finances, you'll get in your life what other people never experience. The tragedy is, more often than not, the financial problems that come in our lives are merely the result of our making wrong choices.

Consequences of Selfishness

In Haggai 1:1 (there's a book you don't hear much about!) we discover some people experiencing a number of problems. And get this, the problems were a direct result of their ignoring God. Specifically, ignoring the things of God and, even worse, the house of God. They were putting their own desires first and ignoring God. Watch the problems they get into. Verses 1-2 say, "In the second year of King Darius, on the first day of the sixth month, the word of the LORD came through the prophet Haggai to Zerubbabel son of Shealtiel, governor of Judah, and to Joshua son of Jehozadak, the high priest: This is what the LORD Almighty says: 'These people say, "The time has not yet come for the LORD's house to be built."'"

Keep that in mind. They'd made a decision. "It's not time to do anything for God yet." Now watch this. "Then the word of the LORD came through the prophet Haggai: 'Is it a time for you yourselves to be living in your paneled houses, while this house remains a ruin?'" (You and I think of paneled houses and don't think they are very nice. But it was nice back then. In fact, they were considered quite nice.)

So God says, "Is it right for you to be living in these lavish, luxurious homes while this house, My house, remains a ruin?" Verse 5 says, "Now this is what the LORD Almighty says: 'Give careful thought to your ways.'" Watch what's about to happen. The financial problems are going to start piling up. "You have planted much, but have harvested little. You eat, but never have enough. You drink, but never have your fill. You put on clothes, but are not warm. You earn wages, only to put them in a purse with holes in it."

Like little gerbils in a cage going around in a circle. It doesn't matter what they do, nothing changes. They work harder, plant more seed, do more stuff, and yet it seems as if they have nothing and aren't getting anywhere. (Remind you of anyone you know?) Something's going on here. Wouldn't you agree?

Look at verse 7: "This is what the LORD Almighty says: 'Give careful thought to your ways. Go up into the mountains and bring down timber and build the house [God's house], so that I may take pleasure in it and be honored.'" Sometimes I run into people who say, "We shouldn't have any church buildings or church facilities. We ought to give all that money to missions." I wonder if these people have a Bible to read, and if they do, have they ever read it? The most phenomenal facility ever constructed on the face of the earth was the temple for which God had given the blueprint. God's the One Who said, "Build Me a house." He says, "Build Me a house so that I may take pleasure in it and be honored." Now watch verse 9, "You expected much, but see, it turned out to be little."

Get the picture? They worked hard, strategized well, and planned carefully. They said, "We're going to be all right. We're going to have a great harvest. Things are going to be great. Everything's going to be wonderful." But in verse 9 God says, "What you brought home, I blew away."

Have you ever gone home and opened up your wallet or pocketbook and said, "Where has my money gone?" Did you know the Bible says money has wings? The Bible says it can fly away. The book of Proverbs says, don't feast your eyes on riches and don't get too attached to riches because they can fly away like a bird (Proverbs 23:5).

"'Why?' declares the LORD Almighty. 'Because of my house, which remains a ruin, while each of you is busy with his own house.'" Here's the key: they got their priorities out of order. "Therefore," God says, "because of you the heavens have withheld their dew and the earth its crops. I called for a drought on the fields and the mountains, on the grain, the new wine, the oil and whatever the ground produces, on men and cattle, and on the labor of your hands."

God says, "You have your priorities all messed up. You put yourself first and not Me. So I shut it all down." I want to make something crystal clear for you. God has the power to do that. When you and I get our priorities out of order, when we put other things or ourselves first, before Him, He'll shut us down. Our financial problems are merely the result of God trying to get our attention. I can guarantee you, every time you and I put ourselves first and put God last, we're headed for trouble. Every time.

Financial problems are to you and your family, your business, and even your church, just like pain sensors in your physical body. God has equipped your physical body with pain sensors. They are there to keep you from destroying your body. God has put pain sensors in my hand so if I hit a wall hard enough, those pain sensors will say, "Don't do that again, dummy!" My brain will say to my hand, "What on earth were you thinking?" My hand will say, "I'm not supposed to think, I'm just a hand." Those pain sensors are God given to keep us from hurting ourselves. Because of His infinite wisdom and because He loves us, God has put pain sensors in our body to keep us from destroying it. Like the warning lights on the dashboard of your car. Pay attention to those warning lights!

Years ago when I was dating my wife, I was driving her car home from Missouri to Tulsa, Oklahoma, when a warning light started flashing on the dashboard. I drove several miles ignoring the warning light, thinking everything would be all right. By the time I pulled over, the engine was blown. It cost us hundreds of dollars to get it fixed because I didn't pay attention to a little warning light on the dashboard that was trying to tell me, "There's a problem, there's a problem, slow down, get off the road, get help!"

Pain Sensors

Warning lights, pain sensors, and financial problems are all designed to get our attention and help us avoid unnecessary trouble. The most insidious disease known to the human body is not cancer and it's not AIDS. The worst disease the body can get is leprosy. Because it systematically destroys all the pain sensors in your body so you can literally run your hand through a wall and not feel it.

Let me tell you what I think is one of the deadliest financial diseases people get: credit. What leprosy is to the human body, credit is to our finances. Credit tells us everything's okay no matter what we do. We may be destroying ourselves, destroying our future, and destroying ourselves financially, but we keep getting these notices in the mail raising our credit limit, telling us we're such wonderful people and can go out and borrow the world. I believe financial problems are God's way of saying to us, "You're not on the right path."

In fact, in Hebrews 12:6 the Bible says He (God) disciplines us because he loves us. God is not about to let you and me walk in rebellion and disobedience and get away with it. So He shuts us down. He gives us financial problems.

Blessings of Obedience

Let me show you another verse: Malachi 3:9. Remember, in Haggai 1 God is the One behind the problems. Here in Malachi, notice God is the One behind the blessings.

Do you see the difference? In Haggai 1 the problems were a direct result of the people ignoring God, specifically the house of God, and putting themselves first. But now in Malachi 3 the blessings are the direct result of people putting God first and tithing. Notice what it says in verses 8-9: "Will a man rob God?" (That's not a very smart thing to do, by the way.) "Yet you rob me. But you ask, 'How do we rob you?' In tithes and offerings. You are under a curse—the whole nation of you—because you are robbing me."

God had shut everything down. In Malachi 3:10, He gives them the answer to getting out of their problems. He says, "'Bring the whole tithe into the storehouse, that there may be food in my house. Test me in this,' says the LORD Almighty, 'and see if I will not throw open the floodgates of heaven and pour out so much blessing that you will not have room enough for it.'" Now watch verses 11-12, "'I will prevent pests from devouring your crops, and the vines in your fields will not cast their fruit,' says the LORD Almighty. 'Then all the nations will call you blessed, for yours will be a delightful land,' says the LORD Almighty."

Don't miss this. God is in control. He's either the One behind our financial problems or the One behind our blessings. And guess who chooses which One He's going to be in our lives? You and I.

Old versus New Testament

Some will undoubtedly say, "That's Old Testament stuff and, Pastor, we don't need to waste our time on the Old Testament because we're a New Testament church." Well, all right, let's go to the New Testament. In 1 Corinthians 10:6, Paul writes, "Now these things occurred as examples to [them]." He's talking about the people in the Old Testament. By the way, you know what an example is, don't you? It's a pattern to follow. Paul says,

> Now these things occurred as examples, to keep us from setting our hearts on evil things as they did. Do not be idolaters, as some of them were; as it is written: "The people sat down to eat and drink and got up to indulge in pagan revelry." We should not commit sexual immorality, as some of them did—and in one day twenty-three thousand of them died. We should not test the Lord, as some of them did—and were killed by snakes. And do not grumble, as some of them did—and were killed by the destroying angel. These things happened to them as examples and were written down as warnings for us, on whom the fulfillment of the ages has come" (1 Corinthians 10:6-11).

In other words you can't just set aside the Old Testament and say, "No, that doesn't have anything to do with me." The whole Bible is for us. And the whole Bible goes together. Sometimes well meaning people will say, "Tithing is an Old Testament concept, and since we're a New Testament church, we no longer have to tithe." All right, let's take that. For the sake of argument let's accept that as a fundamental premise. But I have to ask a question. Did you know there are over 500 prophecies in the Old Testament about the Second Coming of Christ? Can we discard those, too? Do we ignore those? Do we say that those 500 prophecies about the Second Coming of Christ are invalid now because we're New Testament Christians? That would be absurd.

The devil battles people more over baptism and tithing than anything else I know. Did you know that? Want to know why? Because those are starting points in our walk of obedience with Christ.

There are millions of people walking around the earth today, thinking they've been baptized when they really haven't been. "What are you talking about?" You know, the ones who've been sprinkled or had a little bit poured on them, and think they've been baptized. There's not one half of one verse in the Bible that supports that. But they've been told by some denomination, misinformed theologian, church or preacher, it's okay.

Unfortunately it's totally contrary to what the Word of God teaches. The Bible teaches that baptism has to picture the death, burial, and resurrection to be authentic, genuine baptism and only immersion pictures that. (See Romans 6:3-5.) Now follow this. If the devil can mess people up at baptism and keep them from obeying what God said they were to do and they live their whole life walking in disobedience, the devil's won. If he can somehow keep people from knowing what the Bible says they're to do, he's won and we lose.

Next is the tithing issue. Tithing is elementary. It's the starting point for believers. It's not the ending point, it's the starting point. If the devil can hook you by getting you not to tithe and getting you to disobey God in that area of your life, he can rob you of all the blessings God wants to give you. Ironically, once the devil gets you to disobey God in one area of your life, it's that much easier for him to get you to disobey God in other areas of your life as well.

Tithing is in the Old Testament. It really began with Cain and Abel. They were supposed to bring the "first fruits" to God. God evidently had told them, "The best of what you have belongs to Me, bring it to Me." Abel brought the first fruits, the best of what he had, but Cain didn't. God accepted Abel's offering but didn't accept Cain's, and Cain got mad. Do you realize the very first murder in all of human history was over an offering? (It's amazing to me people are still struggling over offerings and giving to God.)

Tithing continued with Abraham long before the Law. He gave tithes to the High Priest Melchizedek in Genesis 14:17-24. Melchizedek was a pre-manifestation of the Lord Jesus Christ.

Remember Jacob's dream of the ladder at Bethel in Genesis 28? He spent the night dreaming of angels coming up and down a ladder and when he woke up in the morning he said, "God has been here." And he promised God, "If you'll bless me, I'll give you a tenth of everything I'll ever receive." This was long before the Law was ever given.

Tithing is also in the New Testament. One of the first passages is Matthew 23:23. I always laugh when someone says they don't think tithing is in the New Testament. Here it is! And guess Who's talking about it? Jesus! Read what He says, "Woe to you, teachers of the law and Pharisees, you hypocrites! You give a tenth [that's a tithe] of your spices—mint, dill and cumin." By the way, those are the three smallest spices known to man. "But you have neglected the more important matters of the law—justice, mercy and faithfulness." What these Pharisees were doing was tithing, even down to the very tiniest spices they had. But they were rude and unjust to people, did not practice mercy, and were not faithful to God. Now watch what Jesus says, "You should have practiced the latter, without neglecting the former." In other words, you should have practiced justice and mercy and faithfulness, but don't neglect your tithing.

It's a whole package. Just because you live a holy life is no excuse not to tithe. And just because you tithe, it's no excuse not to live a holy life. You have to do both. Jesus didn't abolish anything with regard to the Law and the Prophets. In Matthew 5:17-20 He says, "I have not come to abolish any of the Law or the Prophets. I've come to fulfill them" (paraphrase). Do you know what that means? It means He simply came to raise them to a *higher* standard.

Let me show you a contrast between the Old Testament and the New Testament. In the Old Testament they had animal sacrifices. You say, "We don't have that in the New Testament anymore." You're right. We have something better. We have "living sacrifices" (Romans 12:1-2). There are still sacrifices; they're just not dead animals anymore.

In the Old Testament God established the tabernacle and the temple. In the New Testament He established the church. In the Old Testament God said, "Thou shalt not commit adultery." In the New Testament Jesus says, "I tell you that anyone who looks at a woman lustfully has already committed adultery with her in his heart" (Matthew 5:28). For more examples, in the Old Testament they had the Sabbath. In the New Testament we have the first day of the week. In the Old Testament they had the Law and the Prophets. In the New Testament we have the whole Bible and the Holy Spirit. They're not in conflict with each other; they complement each other. The New Testament is the fulfillment, the completion of the Old.

Do you see how Jesus raised things to a higher standard? He didn't abolish anything. He raised them to higher standards.

We've already seen the first two steps on the road to financial freedom.

1. **Acknowledge the sovereignty of God—Attitude.**

2. **Be aware of and avoid the subtlety of debt—Bondage.**

In this chapter we discover step number three: **Adopt the centrality of the tithe.**

If we plan to get out of debt and get rid of our financial problems, the tithe has to be the absolute center of our plan. I'll tell you right up front, the pagan's portfolio does not include tithing, but the Christian's does. The single greatest thing you can do to turn your finances around is to make the choice to start trusting God and start tithing. It will change your life!

EIGHT PRINCIPLES OF TITHING

1. The tithe BELONGS TO THE LORD, not us.

Leviticus 27:30 says, "A tithe of everything ... belongs to the LORD." In Malachi 3:10 God says, "Bring the tithe to Me, to My storehouse." If you study Joshua 7, the story of Achan, you'll find what Achan found out the hard way. You don't mess with the stuff that belongs to God. Study the story of the battle of Jericho. That was the first city they were to conquer in the Promised Land. All the spoils, the first fruits, the tithe, were set apart for the *Lord*. Achan took those spoils for himself. He thought, "God won't miss it; there's so much of it, and I can use this any way I want to." He paid a horrible price for his poor choice. Unfortunately so did his dear wife, his children, every family member he had, and even his animals. He found out the tithe belongs to the *Lord*.

2. We are to BRING the whole tithe into the storehouse.

Malachi 3:10 says we are to *bring* it. The storehouse in the Old Testament was the temple. In the New Testament it's the local church. In Mark 12:41-44 Jesus is with His disciples, and the Bible says they "sat down opposite the place where the offerings were put." You know where that was? The temple. Jesus and the disciples went there and sat down, and evidently no one was fired up about it. It was a very common thing. Everybody knew you were giving.

Occasionally, some people today get nervous when it comes to giving. They'll tell you giving is a private matter between them and God, and no one should know anything about it.

Anyway, when Jesus saw a widow who came and gave her offering, He said, "All these others gave out of their abundance but she gave sacrificially, she gave of all she had" (paraphrase).

We encourage Christians and churches to try online giving. Why? It's simple and, it's better stewardship – for you and for your church. Most people receive their paychecks via direct deposit and pay the majority of their bills online. In fact, many have been doing it for a long time. It eliminates the need for checks, envelopes, postage and time. Even though I've been getting my paycheck via direct deposit for quite some time, I was among the last to begin paying my bills online. I've always been a person who likes to write my own checks, pay my own bills, etc., because I wanted to make sure they got paid. Now, I pay 99 percent of my bills online and can't believe I didn't do it sooner.

Paying bills online is one of the best things I've ever seen. Giving online is too! Every financial institution I know of provides for online giving. It's simple to set up. All you need to do is go online to your financial institution, go to the secure page, and select the tab for paying bills. It will allow you to select merchant accounts. All you have to do is set up a merchant account for your church, put the address and phone number in and you're ready to go.

Next, select the amount. Hopefully, you've already been tithing faithfully. If not, this is a terrific time to start. Calculate 10 percent of your weekly, bi-weekly or monthly paycheck. Then, add an offering to it. For example, if your weekly paycheck is $500, a tithe would be $50. Anything above that is an offering. You might want to give another $5 as an offering. So you would enter $55.00 in the line for the amount. Then, you can select the number of times you want to give. I always select 52 weeks so I am covered for the entire year. (Note: You can change the amount or number of times you want to give at any time through your financial institution.) Once you've entered all the information, you will be shown everything you've entered to make sure it's correct before you finalize the transaction. Once you approve it, you will be all set for online giving for the entire year. This is the ONLY AREA of our Christian life we can make automatic. Once you do, you'll wonder why you didn't do it sooner. And, you can still give something when you come to worship. We'll never out give God. In fact, the Bible makes this promise to the generous: "You'll be made rich in every way so you can be generous on every occasion."

As soon as you get your online giving set up, I'd also recommend you automate your savings. Why? It's simple and it's equally good stewardship. You can do it through your local bank or financial institution. I do ours through The Solomon Foundation. Why? Because they pay the highest rates in the industry. Based in Denver, Colorado, The Solomon Foundation is the fastest growing Christian financial institution and one of the largest in the U.S. You can call them toll free (855-873-5873) and ask how you can set up an account and have funds transferred electronically every week via ACH/EFT. What that means is The Solomon Foundation can set it up with your financial institution where funds can be transferred every week to an account at The Solomon Foundation without your doing anything. You won't have to write a check, spend money on an envelope or stamp, etc. It happens automatically; and whether the amount is $5, $50 or more, each week, you can build a sizable savings each year and do it automatically. Proverbs 13:11 says, "Dishonest money dwindles away, but whoever gathers money little by little makes it grow." We encourage all of our people to automate both their giving and saving by doing it online through their financial institution.

3. We're to bring the WHOLE tithe.

In Malachi 3:10 God said, "Bring the *whole* tithe," all ten percent. Sometimes people, including pastors, make excuses for others and say, "Start with two percent and work your way up." God doesn't tell anybody that. God doesn't say, "Work on it." God doesn't say, "Pray about it." God doesn't say, "See if somehow you can fit that into your budget." That's a lie of the devil. No. God says, "Bring the *whole* tithe."

By the way, we ought to be prepared to give ahead of time. It's Biblical to be prepared to give ahead of time. When we wait until the worship service begins to decide what we're going to give, we're really saying to God and to those around us, "I didn't plan to do anything about this until now." That's one of the reasons I like online giving; it enables you to give your tithe and an offering above your tithe every week, automatically. That way it's planned way ahead of time and giving to God is a pre-arranged priority in our lives. Nothing says you can't give something additional, too, when you come to worship. We do that every week. If you don't do your giving online, make sure it's a part of your regular routine. Decide ahead of time to obey God.

4. We're to bring the whole tithe into the STOREHOUSE.

Again, in Malachi 3:10 notice God says to bring the whole tithe into the *storehouse*, not your house. Did you see that? That's a new revelation for some folks. It doesn't say take God's tithe and use it wherever you need it at your house. John Hagee, Pastor of the Cornerstone Church in San Antonio, has a message on tithing in which he says, "Some of you drove to church today in stolen cars. Some of you are sitting here in the service in stolen clothes. Some of you are living in houses that were built with stolen money. You took God's tithe and used it for yourself."[1] Now I may never be so bold as to say that, but I happen to think he's right. We're not to use God's tithe for our house. It's to be brought to *His house*, the local church, and used for His purposes. It's His tithe.

5. We are to bring the whole tithe into the storehouse ON SUNDAY, the first day of the week.

"Where do you get that?" 1 Corinthians 16:1-2 where the Apostle Paul told the Corinthian church, "Now about the collection for God's people ... On the first day of every week, each one of you should set aside a sum of money in keeping with his income, saving it up, so that when I come no collections will have to be made." The context is a "missionary offering." Paul wants them, when they come together for worship, in addition to the tithes and offerings they receive, to give something in accordance with their income and hold that for this mission offering so when he comes they don't have to take one. Our church does that. For several years we've been developing mission endowment funds. We're saving money in keeping with our income, so when people come to us in need, mission needs, we won't have to take special offerings. That's very Biblical, and it's to be done on the first day of the week, *Sunday.*

By the way, we ought to be prepared to give ahead of time. It's Biblical to be prepared to give ahead of time. When you wait until the worship service to write your check for the offering, you're saying to those around you and to our great God above you, "I didn't plan to do this ahead of time." Someone will say, "Well, that's the way I've always done it." Then change the way you do things and do it at home. Plan to do it. Make it a part of your regular routine. Decide ahead of time to obey God.

6. The tithe belongs to GOD. We are not free to designate it, divide it, or direct it.

The tithe is not yours, the tithe is not mine. It's *God's!* We can't designate it, divide it, or direct it wherever we want it to go. You'd be surprised how many different requests we get in our church. People say, "I want you to take my tithe and use it for this or apply it to that." We can't do that. That's *God's* tithe.

Now it's very Biblical to direct an offering above your tithe. It's interesting how sometimes people will say, "Wow, I can't believe how much money I've given to *God*." I want to say to them, "Go back and figure out what *God's* tithe is, and you'll probably discover you really didn't give that much." You see, the tithe already belongs to Him. We're not giving it to Him, we're giving it back to Him. That's why David said, "[Lord,] who am I, and who are my people, that we should be able to give as generously as this? Everything comes from you, and we have given you only what comes from your hand" (1 Chronicles 29:14). The tithe belongs to *God*.

7. In the Old Testament, priests administered the tithes and offerings. Today CHURCH LEADERS are in charge of that responsibility.

1 Timothy 5:17 says, "The elders who *direct the affairs of the church* well are worthy of double honor"(emphasis added). That's their job. They are to take the tithes we bring, *God's* tithes and our offerings, and they are to use them, and we're to trust them.

8. It's BIBLICAL for leaders to set aside a sum of money from the tithes and offerings of God's people for mission work.

We already saw that in 1 Corinthians 16 and even Philippians 4. We've been doing that in our church for years. Besides the fact we support a large number of missionaries every month, we have also developed seven separate endowment funds. Funds where we have deposited money to earn interest.

Five of these endowment funds are for missions:

1. **The Founder's Fund.** (In honor of the people who started our church.) This fund exists to provide scholarships for people from our church who want to go to Bible college or Seminary.
2. **The Antioch Fund.** This fund exists to provide financial

assistance for people to go on short-term mission trips.
3. **The Philippian Fund.** This fund exists to provide financial assistance for people to go on long-term mission trips.
4. **The Good Samaritan Fund.** This fund exists to provide financial assistance for people who need benevolent help.
5. **The Jerusalem Fund.** This fund exists to provide financial assistance to start new churches.

Because each of these funds has been designated to eventually have over two million dollars, we will never have to touch the principal and can use the interest ("Somebody Else's" money) to fund mission needs from our church until Jesus returns.

Let me share a final thought. Some people have been conditioned to think financial problems are a way of life. That's simply not true. Here's what happens for too many people. Perhaps it's happened to you. When something good happens, you get a raise or a promotion or some unexpected money comes your way, you start thinking, "Oh, this is too good to be true. It won't last. Something bad is coming." Has that ever happened to you?

Here's a verse I hope will become a new life-verse for you. Proverbs 10:22: "The blessing of the LORD brings wealth, and he adds no trouble to it."

How can we get ourselves in a position where God will bless us with wealth and add no trouble to it? 2 Chronicles 26:5 says of Uzziah that "as long as he sought the LORD, God gave him success." What's true of Uzziah will be true of you and true of me. As long as we seek the Lord, as long as we put Him first, God will bless us. The choice is ours.

How do we do that? If we're serious about getting out of debt and getting rid of financial problems, we need to make tithing the centerpiece of our financial planning.

Get this in your head and in your heart. God is the One

behind our financial problems. And God is also the One behind our financial blessings. Once again, here's the promise. If we will bring the whole tithe into the storehouse, God will open the floodgates of heaven and throw out so much blessing that we will not have room enough to receive it (Malachi 3:8-10). Can you think of a better deal than that? I didn't think so.

Remember, we're the ones who determine whether God is behind the burdens or the blessings, the problems or the prosperity. The choice is ours.

FROM THE
GOOD FILE
Simple ideas to encourage you to
GET OUT OF DEBT

Summertime can be a great time to make progress toward your goal of getting out of debt or, if you're not careful, it can be a dangerous time of getting into even more debt. The choice is yours.

The biggest culprit for getting further in debt during the summer months is vacations. Many people will use a credit card to charge plane flights, hotel accommodations, new clothes, meals, and even entertainment expenses with rationalizations: "We deserve this ... we needed a break ... we just had to get away ...", etc. The problem is, you can stack up a small mountain of debt with a one or two-week vacation where you charge everything. The truth is, you'll be paying for your vacation for many months after the memories are long gone and, more often than not, paying with interest, too! (Ouch!)

Action Plans

Here are some suggestions to help you get OUT of debt rather than getting INTO more debt during the summer months:

1. Don't charge anything this summer. Make it a rule you absolutely won't break.

2. Don't buy new clothes just for the summer. Get one more summer out of the ones you have.

3. Have some backyard barbecues instead of going out to eat. (You'll save a lot of money here and won't ever have to stand in line.)

4. Use coupons for your weekly grocery shopping. You can save a lot with coupons.

5. Make a concerted effort to conserve on electricity and water during the summer months. (You don't have to have it like an icebox inside or all green outside. Once-a-week watering is

plenty.)

6. Have a garage sale. (You'll end up with a cleaner garage and some extra money for your family.)

7. Encourage every member of your family to live within his/her means. In other words, always spend less than you earn, and put something in savings each week.

Not only will these things help you have a better summer, they'll also help you **Get Out Of Debt!**

CHAPTER 4

DECISION

*"You don't make decisions because they are easy;
you don't make them because they are cheap;
you don't make them because they're popular;
you make them because they are RIGHT."*
—Theodore Hesburgh

Solomon wrote in Proverbs 13:7, "One man pretends to be rich, yet has nothing; another pretends to be poor, yet has great wealth." There's a verse that describes people in America. In their best selling book, *The Millionaire Next Door*, Thomas Stanley and William Danko shared several shocking revelations. They said that most millionaires buy their suits off the rack. Most millionaires purchase and drive used cars. Most millionaires shop at Sears. Most millionaires make their kids earn their money rather than just giving it to them. And most millionaires always live well below their means. That's why they're millionaires. Unfortunately the majority of people in America are not millionaires. And if they continue their current spending habits, they never will be.

Several years ago *The Fort Worth Star Telegram* ran a series of articles on money and finances. Here's a quote from one of those:

With the economy booming Americans have been on a buying binge and they've got the bulging credit card balances to prove it. Consumer debt, or debt other than mortgages, rose to $1.344 trillion in 1998 from $1.096 trillion in 1995. According to the Federal Reserve, the average American household carries a $2,800 balance each month on credit cards. But many are much more than that. Last year more than 24,000 people visited the Consumer Credit Counseling Service of Greater Fort Worth and west Texas' 28 offices to get help managing their debt. The typical client in our area owed $23,703 on ten credit cards.

"The people I see didn't realize how much they were spending," says Kay Warden, a debt counselor at CCCS's office in Burleson. "They filled out credit card applications at Foley's and other stores without adding it up and if I asked them how much they spent on Christmas, they had no idea."[1]

Obviously financial problems can be incredibly complex. However getting out of a money mess is merely a matter of following some simple steps. So far we've seen the first three steps to achieve financial freedom:

1. **Acknowledge the sovereignty of God—Attitude.**
2. **Be aware of and avoid the subtlety of debt—Bondage.**
3. **Adopt the centrality of the tithe—Choice.**

In this chapter I want to examine the fourth step on the road to financial freedom: **we need to accept God's plan and enjoy the security of obedience—Decision**.

I want to share a story with you from 2 Kings 5:1-15. Even though it's in the Old Testament and it's not about finances or money, there's some great wisdom we can apply to every area of our lives, especially our finances.

NAAMAN THE LEPER

The story begins in 2 Kings 5:1,"Now Naaman was commander of the army of the king of Aram. He was a great man in the sight of his master and highly regarded, because through him the LORD had given victory to Aram. He was a valiant soldier, [watch these next four words] but he had leprosy."

Remember, the most insidious disease the human body can ever contract is leprosy because you lose all of your pain sensors. Verses 2-15:

> Now bands from Aram had gone out and had taken captive a young girl from Israel, and she served Naaman's wife. She said to her mistress, "If only my master would see the prophet who is in Samaria! He would cure him of his leprosy."
> Naaman went to his master and told him what the girl from Israel had said. "By all means, go," the king of Aram replied. "I will send a letter to the king of Israel." So Naaman left, taking with him ten talents of silver, six thousand shekels of gold and ten sets of clothing. The letter that he took to the king of Israel read: "With this letter I am sending my servant Naaman to you so that you may cure him of his leprosy."
> As soon as the king of Israel read the letter, he tore his robes and said, "Am I God? Can I kill and bring back to life? Why does this fellow send someone to me to be cured of his leprosy? See how he is trying to pick a quarrel with me!"
> When Elisha the man of God heard that the king of Israel had torn his robes, he sent him this message: "Why have you torn your robes? Have the man come to me and he will know that there is a prophet in Israel." So Naaman went with his horses and chariots and stopped at the door of Elisha's house. Elisha sent a messenger to say to him, "Go, wash yourself seven times in the Jordan, and your flesh will be restored and you will be cleansed."
> But Naaman went away angry and said, "I thought that he

would surely come out to me and stand and call on the name of the LORD his God, wave his hand over the spot and cure me of my leprosy. Are not Abana and Pharpar, the rivers of Damascus, better than any of the waters of Israel? Couldn't I wash in them and be cleansed?" So he turned and went off in a rage.

Naaman's servants went to him and said, "My father, if the prophet had told you to do some great thing, would you not have done it? How much more, then, when he tells you, 'Wash and be cleansed'!" So he went down and dipped himself in the Jordan seven times, as the man of God had told him, and his flesh was restored and became clean like that of a young boy.

Then Naaman and all his attendants went back to the man of God. He stood before him and said, "Now I know that there is no God in all the world except in Israel. Please accept now a gift from you servant."

Now Naaman was the commander of the army of the king of Aram (Syria). He was highly respected and a valiant soldier, but he had leprosy. From his life and situation there are at least six powerful lessons we can learn that have direct application to our finances.

Six Powerful Lessons

Lesson #1: No one is immune from problems.

It doesn't matter whether you are the commander of an army or the CEO of a corporation or the staff member of a major church. No one's immune from problems. Naaman had leprosy. What's your problem?

Lesson #2: God will use the most unlikely sources to get us what we need.

In Naaman's situation it was a servant girl God used to lead him to the cure of his problems.

Lesson #3: The answer to our problems won't usually be what we want to hear.

Isn't that interesting? It won't usually be what we *want* to hear. Elisha told Naaman, "Go down and dip yourself seven times in the Jordan River."

Lesson #4: We'll be tempted to come up with our own plan.

Too often God tells us to do something in a certain way and we'll say, "Yeah, okay, but I'm going to try it this way." Or we'll try to modify what He tells us. Naaman got angry at what he'd been told and came up with his own plan. He said, "The rivers Abana and Pharpar are far nicer than any of the rivers of Israel." Ever know someone like that?

Lesson #5: Wise friends will always encourage us to do what God says.

One of the surest ways you can tell true friends is: they will always tell you what you need to hear, not what you want to hear. Naaman's friends went to him and his servants went to him, and they encouraged him to do what the prophet told him to do.

Lesson #6: God's way is always the right way.

Naaman eventually did what he was told and was healed. There is great security in obedience. You're never going to obey God and regret it. I've never been around anyone, at the end of their life after following God and being faithful to God, who says, "I sure wish I hadn't been a goody-two-shoes. I wish I hadn't done all the right things. I wish I hadn't lived a holy life. I wish I hadn't done everything I could for God." You know what I have heard, though, hundreds and hundreds of times? "If I could do it all over again, I'd sure do things a whole lot differently. I would have lived for God. I wish I would have followed God's plan."

Let me tell you something about obedience. Obedience always requires two things and there's no exception to this.

Number one is faith. Obedience to God will always require faith on our part. Faith literally means, "Can I trust God to do this? Do I have the faith to trust God? This sounds unbelievable. I don't know how this would ever work. God's calling me to do something, but can I trust God to do this?" It takes faith. The issue is: am I willing to trust God and do it His way?

Number two is faithfulness. Obedience requires our faithfulness. You have to ask, "Can God trust me to do this?" In other words, am I willing to hang in there and see this through to the end?

We're all real good at starting out doing the right stuff. Every January millions of people go through their annual ritual of making New Year's resolutions and all kinds of new commitments. It's a time when we all want to start out right. But so many times we don't even get to the middle of February and we've already blown the commitments we made at the beginning of the year. It takes faithfulness—will you and I hang in there and see this through to the end?

BE PREPARED

When you decide to get out of debt and get your finances in order, at least three things will happen:

1. When you make the decision to follow God's plan, you are going to get discouraged.

You need to know up front you're going to get discouraged. You're going to see other people buying new cars, buying new clothes, and putting additions on their homes. Your neighbors are going to come back from Cancun after a week of vacation and those kinds of things will discourage you. You'll be tempted to say, "Why am I doing all this? Why am I disciplining myself? Why am I going without to get out of debt when they look like they're really happy?" Be prepared ahead of time. There are going to be some discouragements coming your way.

2. You're going to get distracted.

There are going to be some things that come along and you're going to find yourself rationalizing, "We have to get the car fixed and the kids want to go on their school trip and we all need new shoes," etc. The distractions will come, and if you don't watch it, your rationalizations can be pretty convincing. You'll get clear off track and the devil will get you right back in that same bondage again.

3. There will be detractors.

There will always be people who make fun of you. My biggest attacks when we were trying to get out of debt came from co-workers and family members. (Not my immediate family. I told them they could move out if they didn't like the way we were doing things.) But I can't control those friends or family members who always have "a better way of running your life than you do." Sometimes it's your family; sometimes it's your friends; sometimes it's the people you work with. They'll say things to you and their arguments can sure sound good. Before you know it, you can almost convince yourself they're right and you must be wrong. Be prepared for that ahead of time so you can stay on target with your goal of getting out of debt and being free from financial stress.

CALLED TO THE RIGHT WAY

In October, 1999, our church had some tremendous financial needs—getting out of debt and building facilities. So we'd prayed as a leadership about what we should do. We had a number of capital stewardship companies contact us. Big finance consulting firms contacted us for the better part of three years, saying, "We can help your church. What you need to do is have a capital stewardship campaign and get your people to commit the money you need." I'll admit, I've always felt uncomfortable with capital stewardship campaigns. But we went ahead anyway and thought, "We're going to be out of debt and probably should go ahead and do this."

We signed a contract with a professional fund-raising company. The guy came and met with us, and in the first meeting there was an obvious uneasiness. I couldn't explain it but I knew something wasn't right. Following that meeting several of the people who'd been present asked me, independently of the others, why we were using a professional fund-raising company in the first place. A couple of them said, "You ought to do our campaign. You're telling the guy what we ought to do. Why do we need him?"

So I thought, "Maybe I need to back off and not say anything in the next meeting." The next meeting came, and this time those in the meeting were much more resolute in their objections. They said, "We don't think we ought to be doing this." As I listened to those involved in the meetings, I had a disturbing thought. "Is this the servant girl of Naaman here? Do I want to do things my way when God has another way He wants us to go? Do I need to listen to these people because God wants us to do it a different way?" I decided to fast and pray, and as I did, God made it very clear to me, "You need to help get the people in the church out of debt first. Then you'll have all the money you'll ever need for all the things I will tell you to do."

We got out of the contract with the capital fund raising company. Although it cost us a few thousand dollars to do so, to this day we believe we made the right choice.

A couple of months later, the whole issue of debt was weighing heavily on my heart when I went home that December evening after work and showed my wife the Christmas bonus the elders had given us. I asked her what she wanted to do with it, and she suggested we use it to pay off some of the bills we had accumulated.

I quickly determined we had more bills than bonus and, in anger (yes, I know pastors aren't supposed to show emotion but I was angry), I pushed all the bills off onto the floor and told my wife I was tired of "living like this" (driven by debt and living in debt). I stomped upstairs to try to regain my composure. After a few minutes I returned downstairs to the kitchen where I saw the bills still lying on the floor. I picked them up and headed to the church.

I went to my office and got all the books I had in my library on finances and debt and got a book by Larry Burkett called *Debt-Free Living*. When I opened it, I noticed the date at the top of the book. (When I read a book I always write the date I begin to read it in the top right-hand corner.) I had written "7/31/89." Suddenly I remembered what was going on back in 1989. I was pastoring a church in Florida. We were showing a series of videos by Larry Burkett. Every night we showed them, the place was packed. People were interested in getting out of debt and learning how to get out of their financial messes. Everybody I knew was in there. Young couples, older folks, it was wall-to-wall people.

We were watching Larry Burkett teach on how to get out of debt. As a result of that series, Janis and I made some serious commitments. We got rid of cable TV, we stopped the newspaper, we stopped going out to eat, we started eating sandwiches for lunch, and things were going great. At the time we were miserably in debt, but thanks to applying God's principles, we paid off both our cars and every credit card we had. All we had left was the mortgage on our home. It was a miracle that God was getting us out of debt. We were making extra principal payments on our house and were in the process of paying it off. It was a great time in our lives. I even told some friends, "I lived like a king back in the '80s."

After looking at that book in my office, remembering what it was like back in 1989, I added up all our current bills. (Remember now, it's December of 1999—ten years later.) I got my calculator out and began to add it up. As I added, I realized that now, ten years later, we were twice as much in debt as we were in 1989. We looked more successful, lived in a nicer home, drove nicer cars, wore nicer clothes. But, in ten years we were in much worse financial shape than we had been in 1989. Unfortunately, although it looked as if we'd made progress and were actually doing much better, the truth was, we were doing much worse.

As I sat there and considered that in the next two years I would have two of my children in college, I uttered something intensely spiritual, "This is nuts!" And (are you ready for this?) it hit me. Having all the best books on money and finances won't help me. Having all the right principles and all the best CD/DVD series and getting excited about the messages; none of that's going to do it. We have to make a decision, and we have to make a decision now!

I made a fresh commitment before God. "I'm going to apply these principles, I'm going to get back to doing the right things in our finances, and I'm going to stick with it no matter what."

I got my family together for what we affectionately call a "come to Jesus" meeting, and I said, "Guess what, ladies and gentlemen, and children. We're getting out of debt! And there's going to be some changes around here." We had a whole series of "come to Jesus" meetings with our family, many of them impromptu, many at a much higher decibel level than normal. And my family finally got it. They realized how serious I was about this and that I wasn't backing down. So our family made the commitment to get debt free!

When I went back to my office, I put that book by Larry

Burkett (with the 1989 date written in it) on top of my computer because I wanted to have a daily reminder that I would never again go backward financially. I was going to get out of debt. God's principles do work. But I have to put them to work in my life. It's just like Jesus said, "You will know the truth, and the truth will set you free" (John 8:32). It's not the truth that sets you free, it's when you know it that it sets you free. We all have Bibles, but just setting them on the coffee table is not enough. We have to apply what's in the Bible to our lives. We have to make the decision we're going to do it.

How did we get off track from where we were in 1989? Easy. We got discouraged, got distracted, and listened to the detractors. To be honest, when I saw that date in Burkett's book, I was tempted to stop writing the dates in the front of books when I read them. That's one way to deal with it, but that's like the warning light on the dashboard again. We can disable the light to keep it from blinking, or we can heed the warning and deal with the problem.

God never calls us to the easy way, the lazy way, the inexpensive way or the convenient way. He always calls us to the right way. Our job is to decide to listen. Our responsibility is to obey Him and do what He tells us. When we obey, there is great security in that. When we apply God's principles, God's way, we'll always get God's results.

SEVEN SIMPLE STRATEGIES TO GET OUT OF DEBT

Here are some simple strategies to help you get out of debt and be free forever from financial stress and difficulty.

1. Trust God.

Matthew 6:33 says, "But seek first his kingdom and his righteousness, and all these things will be given to you as well."

2. Tithe.

Without question this is the master key to financial freedom. Every Christian ought to be a faithful, consistent tither. I'll tell you why we haven't been in worse shape than we've been financially. We have always been faithful tithers. Ever since I was a kid, I've been a faithful tither. But tithing alone is not going to do it. You've got to control your spending and do the other things God says as well.

I want to extend a challenge to every business owner who reads this book. Every Christian ought to be a tither and every business owner ought to be tithing his personal income. But let me challenge you to go "the second mile" as a business owner. I challenge you to tithe your business income as well. You may ask, "Why should I do that?" Because I've seen what it has done to our own church since we made that decision.

Every leader in our church, every elder, every deacon, every small group leader, every member of our staff are tithers. But you know what? We also tithe what's given in the offerings on Sundays. Since we've done that, which has been years ago now, God has phenomenally blessed our church. The same blessing that's available to us personally is available corporately to a body. In fact, I won't support any parachurch organization or any ministry that does not tithe. Why? Because if an individual can be under a curse for not tithing, a ministry can be under a curse as well (Malachi 3:9).

I want to challenge you to consider that. The same blessings you enjoy personally from tithing can be yours corporately as you tithe from your business income. Think what would happen in our churches if every businessperson in America started tithing their business income this week? Will you lead the way?

3. Develop a Budget.

Luke 14:28-29 says, "Suppose one of you wants to build a tower. Will he not first sit down and estimate the cost to see if he has enough money to complete it?" Do you understand what Jesus was saying? "Won't this tower builder put together a budget? Won't he put together a written plan?" Luke continues, "For if he lays the foundation and is not able to finish it, everyone who sees it will ridicule him, saying, 'This fellow began to build and was not able to finish.'" Jesus encouraged planning, preparing and strategizing.

 a. **You need to develop a "GOOD File."** What's a "GOOD File?" G-O-O-D stands for: Get Out Of Debt. Every time I heard the word "good" or I heard someone say something's good, I was reminded, Get Out Of Debt. That's the reminder I needed to get out of debt. Develop a "GOOD File."

 b. **Both husband and wife need to see the whole picture on a regular basis.** If you'll look at your debt and your bills on a regular basis, it will seriously curtail your spending. Trust me. Too often the wife handles the bills or the husband pays the bills and their mate doesn't see them. So they keep spending, getting further and further in debt, and the wife who's struggling to pay everything or the husband who's struggling to pay everything doesn't want to hurt their mate's feelings and say, "No, we really can't afford that." So you get deeper and deeper in debt, and it's because you didn't take an honest look at your financial situation on a weekly basis.

 c. **I would recommend you read and listen to everything you can on getting out of debt.** I'm always encouraged by the people in our church who are already out of debt who always look forward to the next sermon series on finances or the newest book on effective money management. Someone might ask, "If you're already out of debt, why would you want to hear and read things about getting out of debt?" I think the answer is simple: So you stay out of debt.

4. Get Out Of Debt.

Proverbs 22:7 says, "The rich rule over the poor, and the borrower is servant to the lender." Get out of debt. Stop being a servant to some financial institution. Get out of debt and just be God's servant.

a. **Remember the word INTEREST.** Don't forget what that word really means. If I'm paying interest, "SOMEONE ELSE" is making money; I'm not.

b. **Remember what the letters for DEBT stand for. D-E-B-T:** **D**umb **E**xplanation for **B**uying **T**hings. Remember that. If you have to use debt to buy something, just use those letters, D-E-B-T. It will help encourage you. Or **D**on't **E**ven **B**uy **T**hat if you have to go into debt to get it.

c. **Don't buy anything you can't pay cash for.** If you can't pay cash for it, just wait. We don't like to delay our own gratification. We like to have what we want when we want it—right now. But, friend, you'll either pay now and play later or you'll play now and pay later. If you play now and pay later, you'll pay interest and SOMEONE ELSE will get rich, not you.

d. **Start paying off your debts one at a time.** Start paying them off. It takes discipline to do that. By the way, getting out of debt includes paying off our homes. I've heard people say, "I'm out of debt," and I'll ask, "Is your home paid off, too?" And they'll say, "No. We haven't paid off our home." Then you're not really out of debt. Larry Burkett said, "I advise you to accelerate your mortgage payments to retire the debt as rapidly as possible. I believe one of the essential foundation blocks of a Biblically-oriented financial plan is a debt-free home. This should be the goal of all Christians."[2] Get out of debt.

5. Start saving.

Proverbs 13:11 says, "Dishonest money dwindles away, but he who gathers money little by little makes it grow."

    a. **Always spend less than you earn.** If you'll always spend less than what you get paid every week, you're going to get out of debt, and you're going to get financial freedom in your life.

    b. **Set a goal to have money left over before your next payday.** I get an allowance every week. (Sounds elementary, doesn't it?) My wife gets an allowance every week. My children get an allowance every week. You know what my goal is and the goal I try to teach every member of my family? The goal is to try to get to the next payday with money in your pocket. Then you're ahead of the game. If you keep doing it on a regular basis, you can save up a sizable amount of money and be able to do some nice things with it. For instance, one year I bought Christmas gifts for everyone on my list with cash I'd saved by not spending everything I had every week. My goal is to try to end every week with some extra money in my pocket. It's not that hard, and the benefits are wonderful.

    c. **After you give God's tithe, try to save 10% for yourself.** Pay yourself just like a bill, and put it in savings. This will add up fast.

6. Begin an emergency fund.

Proverbs 6:6-11 talks about the ant and how he stores up things in the summer and Solomon says, "Sluggard, go check out the ant and see how he does it." The Bible is clear we need to be prepared for emergencies.

    a. **Plan for rainy days because somewhere down the road it's going to rain.**

    b. **Don't use your emergency fund to go out to dinner or go**

on vacation. Those are not emergencies; those are indulgences. Have a fund just for emergencies.

c. **You need to have a will**. Find a Christian attorney or a Christian financial planner. Contact them and tell them, "I need to have a will." Don't be one of those who says, "I don't have that much. What do I need a will for?" You need to have a will. One of the best investments you'll ever make is to have a will so you can take care of your family and take care of your children. By the way, I recommend (we've done this in our own will) you tithe 10% of all your assets back to your local church. Why? Because when we're no longer here on this earth, we want God to bless the administration of our assets. This gives us the opportunity, even in our death, to once again acknowledge His sovereign Lordship in our lives and maybe we'd like to have one more opportunity to say, "Thank you, God, for all the financial blessings You've given to our family."

7. Don't quit or turn back.

Don't get sidetracked by what anybody says. Don't allow yourself to be distracted by what happens and don't quit or turn back. In Luke 9:62 Jesus says, "No one who puts his hand to the plow and looks back is fit for service in the kingdom of God." Remember Naaman. The issue wasn't the dipping, it was the obeying. He obeyed God, and God blessed him.

My dream for our church and for churches all across America is twofold. The first is this: To help get every Christian out of debt. The second is: To raise up a generation of people who will be lifetime tithers. Because if I can teach you how to tithe and get you committed to tithing, I can get you "under the spout where the blessings come out," and God will bless you no matter what happens in the days ahead.

FROM THE
GOOD FILE
Simple ideas to encourage you to
GET OUT OF DEBT

Here are some practical tips that will help you enjoy the Christmas holidays and not look back with regret once January gets here.

1. Don't let shopping take priority over worship. If we do, we miss the whole point of Christmas.

2. Don't get caught up trying to outbuy or outdo anybody when you do your Christmas shopping.

3. Don't charge the gifts you buy for others. Yes, you probably won't buy as much, but you won't cry much either later on when the bills come due.

4. Give practical, usable gifts that will help meet needs instead of wasting money on frivolous gifts that will go back in the box, in the closet, the attic, or the next garage sale once the holidays are over.

5. Make sure the Lord is at the top of your Christmas list. (After all, it's His birthday we celebrate.) Giving at your church's Christmas Eve services provides an excellent way to teach your children and model for your family what Christmas is all about.

6. Do take the time to bake Christmas cookies, go see Christmas lights, watch a Christmas video, or some other activity that will help draw your family closer together.

7. Stay on target with your goal to become debt free. Don't allow your emotions and the *spirit of giving* to cause you to get off track and spend what you don't have on things you don't need or have to give.

8. Do take time to thank God for all your blessings and to reflect over the year.

9. Remember the best gift you can give, especially to your own family, is YOU.

Action Plan

Get free from the bondage of financial stress and debt. During the holidays stop by a Christian bookstore and check out the number of excellent resources available on managing your money, practicing Biblical stewardship, and getting out of debt. They'll make great Christmas gifts for your family and friends.

CHAPTER 5

ENCOURAGEMENT

"Here's the bottom line: God says,
'You give Me everything and I'll take care of you.
Or you keep it all and take care of yourself.'"
—John Maxwell

One of the tragic ironies of life is that money and things can never satisfy us. Yet many people are chasing after them with breakneck speed. On the other hand God can satisfy us and take care of everything we need. Yet many people still don't believe it.

Perhaps the following will encourage you.

FIVE CRUCIAL QUESTIONS
ANSWERED BY SCRIPTURE

1. Where do all the resources in the world come from?

Psalm 24:1, "The earth is the LORD's and everything in it, the world, and all who live in it."

2. How can I get those resources?

Deuteronomy 8:18, "Remember the LORD your God, for it is he who gives you the ability to produce wealth ..."

3. When can I get those resources?

Luke 6:38a, "Give, and it will be given to you ..."

4. Who decides how many of those resources I get?

Luke 6:38c, "For with the measure you use, it will be measured to you."

5. Can I ever be free from financial problems?

Proverbs 10:22, "The blessing of the LORD brings wealth, and he adds no trouble to it."

Billy Graham said, "If a person gets his attitude toward money straight, it will help him straighten out almost every other area of his life." Do you have the right attitude toward money? Are you trusting God? It has always amazed me how people are more than willing to trust God for their eternal salvation, but when it comes to their finances they start getting a little nervous. (What's wrong with that picture?)

Martin Luther said, "There are three conversions: the heart, the mind, and the purse." Until we learn to trust God with our money, we aren't really converted. Judging by the average giving of Christians in America (which is now less than 3% of our annual income according to the most recent surveys), there are a lot of unconverted people in our churches.

FIVE REASONS PEOPLE DON'T TRUST GOD WITH THEIR FINANCES

1. Ignorance

They don't know any better.

2. Disobedience

They do know better, but ignore what God says.

3. Selfishness

They don't care what God says and want to keep it all for themselves.

4. Worry

They're scared to trust God and walk by faith.

5. Immaturity

They haven't grown to the place in their relationship with God where they can trust Him to do what He says He will do.

Would you let a thief be president of a bank? Of course not. Then why do we let thieves and robbers lead the church? No one in their right mind would put money in a bank where it was a known fact the president was a thief. Yet far too often, churches allow leaders to remain in positions of leadership who are not faithfully and regularly tithing their income back to God through the local church. Could this help explain, at least in part, the continual plague of financial problems and struggles among our churches?

God is pretty emphatic in Malachi 3 that we are robbing Him when we don't bring the tithe to the storehouse. If every Christian ought to be a tither, and they should (giving at least 10% of your weekly earnings to God), then certainly every leader in the church ought to be a tither as well. In fact, leaders ought to lead the way and be tithers as a matter of public record.

Larry Burkett said,

> The word tithe literally means a tenth. Since this is the minimum amount mentioned in the Bible, it would be logical to assume that it's the minimum amount God wants from a believer. If we can't return even the smallest part to God, it merely testifies that the whole has never been surrendered to Him. In the book of Malachi, the prophet confronted God's people with the fact that they didn't love Him. Yet, they said that they did love Him. But the evidence against them was that they

didn't give. This is the only place in Scripture where God ever told His people to test Him. Plus this passage makes the principle of tithing clear. It's an outside indicator of an inside spiritual condition. It's our testimony that God owns everything in our lives.[1]

If you're not tithing, you ought to start this week as a matter of obedience to God. Not to mention the other benefits that come with it. If you're a leader in a local church or a parachurch organization, you ought to step down from your position of leadership until you begin obeying God in this critical area of your life. Why? In Malachi 3 God says the whole nation was "under a curse" because the people weren't tithing (Malachi 3:9). Like Achan (in Joshua 7), who single-handedly took the blessing off the nation of Israel, you, too, could be placing your church or ministry in a position where God can't bless it because of your disobedience.

Leaders ought to be tithers as a matter of record and as an "example to the flock of which the Holy Spirit has made you overseers" (Acts 20:28). Those who refuse to tithe or to be held accountable for tithing ought not be leaders in God's church or in any organization that represents God.

SEVEN LAWS OF PROSPERITY

You can't violate any of these laws and expect God to bless you financially.

1. The Law of Sowing and Reaping (2 Corinthians 9:6)

"Remember this: Whoever sows sparingly will also reap sparingly, and whoever sows generously will also reap generously." If you don't sow anything, you won't reap anything. You will reap what you sow. You will reap more than you sow, and you will reap later than you sow.

2. The Law of Blessing (Psalm 1:1-6)

Blessed is the man
   who does not walk in the counsel of the wicked
or stand in the way of sinners
   or sit in the seat of mockers.
But his delight is in the law of the Lord,
   and on his law he meditates day and night.
He is like a tree planted by streams of water,
   which yields its fruit in season
and whose leaf does not wither.
   Whatever he does prospers.

Not so the wicked!
   They are like chaff
   that the wind blows away.
Therefore the wicked will not stand in the judgment,
   nor sinners in the assembly of the righteous.

   For the Lord watches over the way of the righteous,
      but the way of the wicked will perish.

Blessing always follows obedience. Don't ever forget that.

3. The Law of Origination (James 1:17)

"Every good and perfect gift is from above, coming down from the Father of the heavenly lights, who does not change like shifting shadows." Deuteronomy 8:18 says, "But remember the Lord your God, for it is he who gives you the ability to produce wealth, and so confirms his covenant ..." It all originates with God.

4. The Law of Generosity (2 Corinthians 9:10-11)

"Now he who supplies seed to the sower and bread for food will also supply and increase your store of seed and will enlarge the harvest of your righteousness. You will be made rich in every way so that you can be generous on every occasion, and through us your generosity will result in thanksgiving to God." God will always be generous to those who are generous to His work.

5. The Law of Determination (Luke 6:38)

"Give, and it will be given to you. A good measure, pressed down, shaken together and running over, will be poured into your lap. For with the measure you use, it will be measured to you." You and I determine the level of our blessings.

6. The Law of Firstfruits (Proverbs 3:9-10)

"Honor the Lord with your wealth, with the firstfruits of all your crops; then your barns will be filled to overflowing, and your vats will brim over with new wine." When we give God our best, our firstfruits, His blessings overflow in our lives.

7. The Law of Trust (Malachi 3:8-10)

"Will a man rob God? Yet you rob me. But you ask, 'How do we rob you?' In tithes and offerings. You are under a curse—the whole nation of you—because you are robbing me. Bring the whole tithe into the storehouse, that there may be food in my house. Test me in this," says the Lord Almighty, "and see if I will not throw open the floodgates of heaven and pour out so much blessing that you will not have room enough for it." It's not a matter of accounting. It's a matter of attitude. Do we trust God?

Sir John Templeton, one of the world's most respected investors and investment counselors, said countless people had asked him over the years, "What's the best investment?" He said he never hesitated to offer this surprising answer: tithing. Here is what Sir John wrote: "In all my fifty-two years before I retired as an investment counselor, we were helping people, literally hundreds of thousands of people, with their wealth. In all of those years there was only one investment which never proved faulty, and that was tithing—giving at least 10% of your income to your church. In all my history I have never seen a family who tithes for as long as ten years that didn't become both prosperous and happy. That is the best investment anyone can select."[2]

Jesus said in Matthew 6:21, "For where your treasure is, there your heart will be also." Do you and I really have a heart for God and the things of God? If we do, our giving will show it.

FROM THE

GOOD FILE

Simple ideas to encourage you to
GET OUT OF DEBT

Implementing a Reward System

One of the best ways to get out of debt is to implement a reward system in your family. Let me share a personal example:

Years ago when we were living in Florida, I'd made the commitment to Janis that we would return to her family's home in Oklahoma every Christmas. (Be careful what you promise, guys.) Obviously it cost a great deal of money each year, especially as our young family was growing. Plane flights, rental cars, Christmas gifts. How did we do it? We charged it on a credit card. Every year. And then we'd spend the rest of the year paying it off.

We did that for several years until one year in the fall I made the announcement we weren't going to do that anymore. I shared with our family that it was nuts to keep charging our vacation, Christmas gifts, etc., on a credit card, and then spend the rest of the year trying to pay it off, plus interest! I announced we would be staying in Florida that Christmas, and if we were able to save up the money to go next year, we'd go.

Well, guess what happened? One year later somehow (miraculously?) we were able to save more than enough money to fly back to Oklahoma from Florida, buy nicer than normal gifts, have some extra spending money on our trip, and even have some left over when we returned home. Oh, and by the way, we've never charged another vacation since.

Action Plan

Implement a reward system. Save up the funds needed ahead of time, and the reward is not only a debt-free vacation but also the reward of not having to pay interest. The reward system works not only for vacations but also for virtually anything else. And it's a GOOD way to manage your resources.

CHAPTER 6

FUNDING

---

*"Stewardship is the use of God-given resources
for the accomplishment of God-given goals."*
—Ron Blue

WE ALREADY HAVE THE RESOURCES

Would you be shocked if I told you God has already provided the funding to completely underwrite every ministry, minister, mission, missionary, and Christian enterprise in the world? Sound far-fetched? I'm not the first one to say it. Here's what Larry Burkett said, "Consider what would happen in America if Christians committed themselves to the Lord. Empty Tomb, Inc., notes that if American church members would increase their giving to an average of ten percent (current estimates are that Christians in America are giving less than 3%), there would be an extra $69 billion for overseas missions."[1] That's just for missions! It's been estimated there would also be an additional $150 billion in income for American churches if we could just get Christians to tithe.

Think of it. No special offerings. No special fund-raising drives. Just Christians simply and faithfully obeying God by bringing the tithe to the storehouse every Sunday here in America.

It would result in an extra $219 billion dollars for the kingdom. It's currently estimated that there are over 350,000 churches in America. That would mean an additional $625,714.29 for every church in America. Could your church use an extra $625,714.29? Absolutely. So how do we get to the place where that can happen? We have to teach our people God's supernatural system for funding His work here on the earth.

Not long ago I heard the story of Sam Houston, the famous renegade from Texas. I'm told this story is true. It seems that as Sam was about to be baptized in a river, the preacher said, "Sam, when I dunk you into the water, all of your sins are going to come out of you and into the water." As Sam Houston reflected on his life of drinking, carousing, womanizing and gambling, he bowed his head. The pastor asked, "Sam, what are you doing?" Sam replied, "I'm saying a prayer for the folks downstream."

Then the pastor said, "Sam, you better take your wallet out of your pocket or it will get soaking wet." To which Sam replied, "Nothin' doin'—if I'm going to be baptized, I want my wallet baptized, too!"

If we're ever going to reach our financial potential in our personal lives, our churches, our ministries, and in our ability to fund worldwide missions' causes, we're going to have to have our wallets baptized, too! Dr. Homer G. Lindsay, former pastor of the famous First Baptist Church in Jacksonville, Florida, said, "I've found, in all my years of ministry, that if people don't get victory when it comes to tithing and giving offerings above the tithe, they don't get victory in the other areas of their lives as well."[2]

When I came to Texas in August of 1992, our church was averaging less than 200 in morning worship, offerings averaged just over $3,300 a week, and the total given to missions (for the year) was $14,366.31. The church also had a considerable amount of debt. Now more than 6,000 people call Crossroads their church home. Our weekly budget is almost $200,000.00 and total missions' giving since then is approaching $10 million.

In 2004 we relocated our ministry to a gorgeous 150-acre campus with a magnificent, 150,000 square foot, first-phase facility. We secured a short-term loan for $15 million and planned to pay it off in seven years. Thanks to the blessing of God and the generosity of our Crossroads' church family, we were able to pay the loan off three years early and declared our financial independence on Sunday, November 9, 2008! We did all that without a capital stewardship campaign or any help from professional fundraisers — just the tithes and offerings of our people.

In 2010 we dedicated our new SportCenter, which includes a huge gym with two basketball courts, fixed seating with backs and armrests, restrooms, a fully functional stage for meetings, programs, etc., large lobby area with concession stand and a gigantic, adjacent amphitheater for outdoor events and programs. There are also six soccer fields, three football fields with lights, four U.S. Open style tennis courts with lights, four sandpit volleyball courts and a large pavilion with outdoor restrooms. And we built all of that without a single dime of debt.

In November of 2011, we began raising funds for a new children's building and a new youth building, both costing $15 million each. In November of 2013, we began construction of our new children's building and it was completely paid for before we broke ground. Now, we are raising the funds for our new youth building and hope to have the funds raised and construction started soon.

What made the difference? We've taught our people God's supernatural system for funding His work in our world: tithing. Is every member of our church a tither? Not yet. But we're headed in that direction. As you can see from the statistics, those who've already learned to trust God by tithing have helped make a phenomenal difference in the funds we have available for our ministry. And we haven't even discussed offerings (giving above the tithe) or what happens when our people get out of debt and our churches get out of debt. Talk about an exponential blessing upon the Body of Christ! There are no limits to what God could do through us if we'd just learn to trust Him in the area of tithing and managing our finances according to the principles of His Word.

Henry Crowell, the founder of Quaker Oats, was so moved by a sermon by Dwight L. Moody that he made a remarkable commitment to the Lord. He said, "Lord, I can't be a preacher, but I can be a good businessman. If you will make me money, I will use it in your services." He gave far beyond the tithe for over 40 years.

William Colgate ran away from home at age 17. He tithed the first dollar he made as an employee. Soon he was made partner of the company and ultimately owned Colgate Palmolive Company. His giving grew from 20% to 30% to 40%, and finally he was giving all of his income to the Lord.

R.G. LeTourneau, creator and manufacturer of giant, earth-moving machinery, by the end of his career reversed the percentages and gave God 90% while he lived on 10%. J.L. Kraft of the Kraft Cheese Company was a tither. Wallace Johnson, the founder of Holiday Inn, was a tither. John D. Rockefeller, Sr., was a tither. J.C. Penney was a tither. Are you? If not, let me challenge you to accept God's challenge and start tithing this week and continue tithing every week for the rest of your life. When you do, you're going to discover that God is a faithful God and He will literally "open the floodgates of Heaven and pour out so much blessing that you don't have room enough for it."

A FOUNDATION YOU CAN BUILD ON

Once we've established tithing as the foundation of our lives and our churches, the possibilities for ministry are limitless. Following are some recommendations of what we should do next.

1. Get out of debt.

a. Personally. Dave Ramsay says, "If you are weighed down with debt, you will have awful difficulty moving forward no matter how strong your vision is. You must get completely out of debt as soon as possible to avoid wasting your most creative time and energies on digging yourself out of a self-imposed pit."[3]

b. Corporately (your church). Jeff Berg and Jim Burgess, in their excellent book, *The Debt-Free Church*, wrote, "Virtually every debt-free ministry we have spoken to in the last several years has been delighted to be debt-free. Pastors, elders, deacons, administrators, and folks in the pews get excited when they are involved in a healthy, well-balanced ministry that is debt-free. The pastor of one of America's largest debt-free churches told us, 'Our people are so thrilled with what we see happening as a result of being out of debt [that] we will never go back to borrowing.' We discovered infectious enthusiasm and creativity in debt-free ministries."[4]

2. Stay out of debt.

Christian financial expert Larry Burkett said, "90% of all church building programs include indebtedness."[5] There's a better way to do it. Several years ago we decided not only did we want to get out of debt as a church, but we wanted to stay out. That meant we would build all future facilities, fund future programs, without long-term debt. Is it possible for a church to do that? Yes. There are a growing number of churches who are doing everything in their ministries without borrowing a dime.

We made the decision to reduce our expenditures in our annual operating budget to the level we were at six years previous in order to dedicate a significant sum of our weekly offerings to paying off our debt and preparing for future expansion. (This is how we got out of debt so fast.) We began with approximately $500 a week our first year. We were able to move it to $5,000 a week the next year. Until we got to the place where we had $75,000 a week set aside for nothing but future expansion. That's $3.9 million a year for nothing but future expansion, and it comes out of our regular, weekly general fund offering. We don't have special offerings. All we ask our people to do is tithe each week and give an offering above the tithe as they are led by God to do so.

Here's how it's worked for us. In 1995 we moved into our new Family Life Center that cost us $1.2 million. We did a capital stewardship campaign with all the bells and whistles. We asked our people to make additional commitments over a three-year period. We printed sharp, four-color brochures. We had a big commitment banquet. We did it all. It took us seven years to raise the funds we needed to pay off our loan, with interest ("Somebody Else" was getting that money, not us!). Seven years!

We decided there had to be a better way to do it. We made adjustments in our budget and in our spending so that now, what used to take us seven years to do before, **with** debt, will only take us a few weeks now **without** debt.

And we're not stopping there. Our goal is to get to the place where $100,000 a week is designated from our general fund offerings for future expansion. That's $5.2 million a year. Think of the possibilities! What could you do for ministry, for missions, with an additional $5.2 million a year? And that's completely above and beyond all of our operating expenses. Sound impossible? It's not. We're already doing it and are well on our way to our goals. You can do it, too. It just takes determination, discipline, and dedication to stick with it.

Depending on the size of your church, you may want to start with $500 a week being designated for debt retirement and future expansion. (That's $26,000 a year.) Or if you can do $1,000 a week, it's $52,000 a year. If you can do $10,000 a week, that's over half a million dollars a year! Start with whatever you can, but stretch as far as you possibly can so you can begin reaping the benefits in your ministry. Then each year simply add to the amount you are designating until your debt is completely eliminated. Once you are debt free, start putting the money on deposit with a financial institution that will pay you interest. (That's right, "SOMEBODY ELSE" will be giving you money to add to the money you have on deposit. What a concept!)

Here's more good news. Did you know it's Biblical for us to do ministry that way? Listen to the words of Moses in Deuteronomy 28:12, "The LORD will open the heavens, the storehouse of his bounty, to send rain on your land in season and to bless all the work of your hands. You will lend to many nations but will borrow from none."

A FUTURE YOU CAN COUNT ON

What's ahead for you personally and for the church of the Lord Jesus Christ? As Christians and churches begin to apply God's simple principles for financial freedom, I believe we are on the verge of seeing the most phenomenal accomplishments in the history of Christianity. The possibilities for ministry and missions are almost beyond comprehension. Things we never before thought an entire denomination might accomplish in a lifetime are now being accomplished by a single local church on a regular basis. We are already seeing a vast movement among the people of God to get out of debt personally and corporately in our churches, and it is opening doors that were mere dreams up until now.

There's another growing movement in the body of Christ that is one of the most remarkable developments we've seen in evangelical Christianity. It's the growing number of huge philanthropic donations being made to churches and ministries here in America.

In 1998 Helen Gantz, age 91, died and left $1 million dollars to her church in rural Indiana. In 1998 Elaine Gabbert, who had lost her mother and husband to death, gave $1.1 million to a Baptist children's home in east Dallas. In December of 1998 Joan Kroc, wife of the founder of McDonald's, Ray Kroc, gave $80 million to the Salvation Army. It was the largest donation in the ministry's 133-year history.

In February of 1999 a 101-year-old man named Christian Thomsen gave $1.1 million to Faith Baptist Bible College and a substantial sum to his local church through his will. In 2000 America Online chairman Steve Case and his wife Jean gave $8.35 million to the Coral Ridge Presbyterian Church and Dr. D. James Kennedy to help them with their Christian school. Last year Warren Bailey left $60 million to his local church in St. Mary's, Georgia.

The historic First Baptist Church of Dallas, where for many years the beloved W.A. Criswell served as pastor, has entire buildings donated by families who were members of their church. The great Prestonwood Baptist Church in Plano, Texas, began to experience phenomenal growth a number of years ago when Mary Kay Ash (Mary Kay Cosmetics) donated a huge sum for them to build a new building at a crucial time in their history.

In May of 2001 Dr. Tim LaHaye and his wife, Beverly, gave a dramatic $4.5 million dollar donation to Dr. Jerry Falwell and Liberty University in Lynchburg, Virginia. Dr. LaHaye is a renowned pastor, theologian, and author. Another donor who requested anonymity gave another $4.5 million dollar donation bringing the total to $9 million.

In the days ahead I believe we are getting ready to witness even more phenomenal gifts given to churches and ministries all over the world. God has given the resources to us so there will always be more than enough to reach the world with the gospel. It's just a matter of our listening to His voice and obeying His Word.

People all over the world are realizing God has blessed them to amass significant fortunes not just for the sake of accumulating vast sums of wealth, but rather to help fund His kingdom work on the earth before Jesus returns. Let me challenge you to evaluate where you are today and what God has blessed you with and ask you to consider being one of those Christian philanthropists who blesses the socks off a church or a ministry somewhere in the world. I challenge you to help your local church first, and then ask your pastor for ideas of other ministries you can help.

If we enthusiastically and consistently apply God's simple principles for financial freedom to our lives and to our churches, the day will come when we can all do it.

Just remember the A, B, Cs!

FROM THE
GOOD FILE
Simple ideas to encourage you to
GET OUT OF DEBT

The Priority of Saving

Contrary to what many Christians have been led to believe, saving money is both Biblical and practical. Solomon wrote in Proverbs 13:11, "Dishonest money dwindles away, but he who gathers money little by little makes it grow."

Saving money is both Biblical and practical. And the discipline of saving something from each paycheck will provide benefits and blessings you will be grateful for the rest of your life.

Ironically it's rarely the theological ramifications that hold people back from saving. Rather it's just plain procrastination. We plan on getting started—just not today.

Years ago I heard the following slogan: "If not now, when? If not here, where? If not you, who?" Those are good questions to ask when it comes to saving.

- ➤ "If not now, when do you plan on saving?" (There's no better time than right now.)
- ➤ "If not here, in your present job and in your present location, where will you begin?"
- ➤ "If not you, who's going to do it for you?" (Answer? No one.)

Even if you can only start with $5 or $10 a week, you ought to start saving today. Your ultimate goal should be the 10-10-80 plan (i.e., 10% to God, 10% to savings, and 80% to live on).

Consistent, regular savings each week over a long period of time is one of the smartest ways you can stop working for money and have your money work for you. But don't take my word for it, take Solomon's, who said that "he who gathers money little by little makes it grow."

That's GOOD advice ... for all of us.

Action Plans
 A. Make the commitment to yourself, your family, and God that you will start saving. Begin with your next paycheck.

 B. To motivate you as you save, set some goals. Dream a little and decide some short and long term goals for your savings.

 C. Rejoice in the Lord as you are able to meet these goals.

ENDNOTES

Chapter One

1. *Fort Worth Star Telegram*, 25 December 1999. Copyright 1999, *Fort Worth Star Telegram*.
2. Brochure from Christian Financial Concepts, 1999. Used by permission.
3. Larry Burkett, *Debt-Free Living* (Chicago: Moody, 1989), p. 58.

Chapter Two

1. Paul and Veva Young, January, 2000. Used by permission.
2. Mark and Vera Strickland, January, 2000. Used by permission.
3. C. Peter Wagner, *Churchquake* (Ventura, CA: Regal Books, 1999), pp. 243-244.
4. Ibid.
5. Larry Burkett, *Debt-Free Living*, p. 57.
6. Mary Hunt, *Debt-Proof Living* (Nashville: Broadman & Holman, 1999), pp. 65-66.
7. Ibid., p. 11.

Chapter Three

1. John Hagee, from the tape, "Twelve Principles of Prosperity," John Hagee Ministries, 1999. Used by permission.

Chapter Four

1. Article in *Fort Worth Star Telegram*, 16 January 2000. Copyright 2000, *Fort Worth Star Telegram*.
2. Larry Burkett, "Questions and Answers," Web site article, Christian Financial Concepts, January 18, 2000. Used by permission.

Chapter Five

1. Larry Burkett, *Answers to Your Family's Financial Questions* (Pomona, CA: Focus on the Family, 1987), pp. 106-107.
2. Gary Moore, *Ten Golden Rules for Financial Success* (Grand Rapids: Zondervan, 1996), pp. 141-142.

Chapter Six

1. Larry Burkett, *Christian Financial Concepts Newsletter*, January, 2001. Used by permission.
2. Dr. Homer G. Lindsay, former pastor of First Baptist Church in Jacksonville, Florida. Used by permission.
3. Dave Ramsay, *How to Have More Than Enough* (New York: Penguin, 2000), p. 78.
4. Jeff Berg and Jim Burgess, *The Debt-Free Church* (Chicago: Moody, 1996), pp. 15-16.
5. Ibid., p. 119.

SAMPLE BUDGET
FOR GETTING OUT OF DEBT

The next five pages present a simple budget consisting of five elements *anyone* can use.

1) **A *financial overview* of three things:**
   - (1) remaining *debt*
   - (2) current *savings*
   - (3) unpaid *bills*

2) **Annual expenses and obligations in detail**

3) **A *weekly expense* budget that guides spending**

4) **A *monthly expense* budget detailing obligations**

5) **Retirement accounts updating the growth of funds**

Don't use the word "budget" if you don't want to. Call it your "**GOOD File**." It is your get-out-of-debt plan, and it will keep you on track toward your financial goals. Simply plug in *your own* numbers and totals, and you're ready to go. Keep it updated weekly on your computer and also file a hard copy.

Every week print a copy of page one. If you're married, share this with your mate so you are both always aware of the obligations you have and the progress you are making. This will serve as an ongoing motivation for you to get out of debt as quickly as possible.

Getting Out of Debt
Financial Overview

A. Remaining Debt as of 12/27/13

$22,470.72	GMAC (Bob's car)
18,999.60	TMC (Carla's car)
3,815.00	Mastercard
2,756.16	Upland Motorsports
1,670.50	VISA
$49,711.98	**(Total remaining debt)**

B. Savings as of 12/27/13

$1,500.00	First Federal (Emergency Fund) Account #79832-293

C. Outstanding Bills as of 12/27/13

$ 557.00	Rent/Mortgage Payment
468.14	Bob's car payment
316.60	Carla's car payment
229.68	Waverunner payment
151.33	Car Insurance
$1,722.75	**(Total)**

Getting Out of Debt
Annual Expenses
as of 12/27/13

Annual Income: $66,719.64 (1,283.07 per week gross)
Approximate Disposable Income: $55,780.00
　　　(1,072.69 per week net)
Savings Goal: $1,040.00 ($20.00 per week)

Annual Expenses:

$ 6,672.00	Tithe
1,040.00	Savings
6,684.00	Rent/House payment
$ 1,260.00	Electric
1,800.00	Gas
600.00	Water
420.00	Cable
248.50	Internet
780.00	Phone
600.00	Cell phone
300.00	Long distance phone
$ 6,500.00	Groceries
520.00	Dry cleaning
$ 200.00	Renter's/Homeowner's insurance
1,825.96	Car insurance
120.00	Waverunner insurance
1,500.00	Health insurance
$ 5,617.68	Bob's car
3,799.92	Carla's car
600.00	Car maintenance
2,756.16	Waverunner payment
2,400.00	Mastercard
1,200.00	Visa

$ 520.00	Girls' allowance
2,080.00	Carla's allowance
2,080.00	Bob's allowance
600.00	Clothes allowance
600.00	Miscellaneous/Entertainment
800.00	IRA
1,000.00	401K
$55,124.22	**(Total÷52=1,060.08 per week)**

Getting Out of Debt
Monthly Expenses
as of 12/27/13

A. Weekly Income: $1,283.07

$ 173.07	Child support
700.00	Bob's salary
410.00	Carla's salary
$1,283.07	**(Total)**

B. Fixed Weekly Expenses:

$128.30	Tithe
20.00	Savings
40.00	Bob's allowance
40.00	Carla's allowance
125.00	Groceries
10.00	Girls' allowance
10.00	Dry cleaning
$373.30	**(Total)**

C. Amount left for other weekly expenses and obligations:

$909.77 (gross)
$699.39 (net)

Getting Out of Debt
Weekly Expenses

A. Monthly Expense Budget:

$55,124.22 divided by 12=$4,593.68
(Please see "Annual Budget" on pages 133–134)

B. Monthly Credit Card/Loan Payments:

$229.68	Waverunner
200.00	Mastercard
100.00	VISA
$529.68	

C. Total Monthly Net Income:

C. Total Monthly Net Income:	**$4,644.74**
Total Fixed Monthly Expenses:	4,590.14
Difference	$ 54.60

Getting Out of Debt
Retirement Funds
as of 12/27/13

IRAs $31,150.88
                        (Account #290342-392
                          and #290342-393)

401K $28,140.34
                        (Account #189204)

Total Retirement: **$59,291.22**

BLOGS
by Barry L. Cameron

TRAPPED

For three days, off the coast of a desolate Russian peninsula called Kamchatka, seven crew members of a small Russian AS-28 mini submarine huddled together and hung on for life. Their vessel, running dangerously short on oxygen, was literally strapped to the Pacific Ocean floor some 600 feet below the surface.

The vessel had gotten entangled in fishing nets and a cable that is part of the Russian coastal monitoring system. Crew members moved into a single compartment of the forty-four-foot long, miniature sub and minimized their movements to conserve oxygen. 40-degree temperatures and a buildup of noxious gas inside the submarine made them drowsy and actually enabled them to conserve energy and air.

Five years ago, a similar incident took place with a Russian sub. In August of 2000 it was a nuclear submarine called the Kursk. It went down in the Barents Sea and all 118 crewmen on board died. Ironically, those men probably could've been saved. But Russian leaders refused all offers of help fearing the compromising of military secrets and a perception of national weakness. Numerous proposals of international help were refused until all hope had been virtually exhausted. By then it was too late.

This time, Russia moved quickly to ask for help. Calling upon the United States and Great Britain, among others, every effort was made to save the seven submariners trapped on the bottom of the ocean floor. Rescue teams were immediately dispatched with state-of-the-art equipment, a cash-strapped Russian navy apparently can't afford, for such deep sea rescue operations.

A British remote-controlled submarine was able to cut away the cable and the fishing nets that had ensnared the Russian mini-sub, allowing it to surface. All seven crew members crawled out of the hatch on Sunday, August 7th, weak but very relieved to be back on the surface again. Rescuers said they barely had six hours of oxygen left when the sub surfaced.

Two Russian submarines. Two radically different results: one tragic, one triumphant. Why? This time the Russian government wasn't afraid to ask for help.

Are you trapped today because you're afraid to ask for help? Like a student in a school classroom afraid to raise your hand and ask the question everyone else needs answered because they fear what others will say or think? If you don't ask for help, you won't get it. What's worse, the results can be tragic.

The Bible clearly says, "If any of you lacks wisdom, he should ask God, who gives generously to all without finding fault, and it will be given to him" (James 1:5). Jesus said, "Ask and it will be given to you; seek and you will find; knock and the door will be opened to you. For everyone who asks receives; he who seeks finds; and to him who knocks, the door will be opened" (Matthew 7:7-8).

Billy Graham said, "Heaven is full of answers to prayers which no one ever bothered to ask."

You know what's worse than being trapped on the ocean floor in a totally dark, terrifyingly cold submarine thinking you're about to die?

Being afraid to ask God for help.

WAIT A MINUTE!

Sunday, December 17, 2000, was one of the bloodiest days in the history of Italy. And the Mafia had nothing to do with it. It happened in the Italian Alps when a cold spell coated the mountainsides with a sheet of ice that proved deadly for a group of climbers. One after another, an Italian climber, his dog, and three others who tried to rescue them, fell some 1600 feet to their deaths.

It all began when Luigi Lazzaretti, who had been hiking with his two huskies Sasha and Zara, happened upon one of the ice-covered slopes. Sasha slipped, and instinctively, Luigi tried to catch his dog. As he did, he lost his footing and started the fatal descent down the side of the mountain, taking his other huskie, Zara with him.

Within minutes, a witness said, all you could hear were people shouting for Luigi and calling for someone to help. A man known for his expert climbing abilities was quickly summoned. Unfortunately as he attempted to help, he fell to his death. Another man tried to help as well as another after him. Tragically both of them plunged to their deaths.

"There was a chain of the dead," recounted Danilo Barbiscotti, who took part in the failed rescue effort on the 7,920-foot high Mount Arera. When the trained Alpine rescuers finally arrived to the pile of bodies at the bottom of the slope, ironically it was Sasha, the original huskie who'd slipped, who was still alive.

Now get the picture. Four men fell to an absolutely un-necessary death all because they got in a hurry and felt they needed to do something. The cold reality of the matter is that all they really needed to do was simply wait. One of the rescuers recounted, "As we were trying to get the first climber, we saw the others falling."

Honestly none of us like to wait. We don't like to wait in line. We don't like to wait for our food. We don't like to wait at the bank. We don't like to wait anywhere for anything. Period. We don't even like to wait on God.

So listen carefully. Before you get out on the slippery slopes that will most certainly lead to a calamitous conclusion: better wait a minute. You've got nothing to lose by controlling your impetuous impulses. Especially when it comes to God. Because He's always on time and always has your best interest at heart. All you need to do is wait.

"They that wait upon the LORD shall renew their strength; they shall mount up with wings as eagles; they shall run, and not be weary; and they shall walk, and not faint" (Isaiah 40:31, KJV).

BEWARE THE ELEPHANT SMUGGLERS

Officials in Mexico are still trying to figure out how they did it. Somehow someone was able to sneak "Benny" across the border at the Matamoros checkpoint. Ordinarily it wouldn't make the news. After all, smuggling of one kind or another happens almost on a daily basis between the United States and Mexico. But since "Benny" is a 9-year-old, Indian elephant who weighs 3 tons and stands 10 feet tall, Mexican authorities are steaming about it. Especially when it was discovered that "Benny" came across the border into Matamoros in a wooden box on a flatbed truck.

Guillermo Vazquez, one of the owners of the circus where "Benny" has been performing in Mexico, said he bought the elephant in Houston for $40,000.00 and sought all the proper papers for export. He became frustrated with all the red tape, bureaucracy, and delays and decided to hire a "coyote" (a professional smuggler) to sneak the elephant into Mexico.

"He's a very nice elephant," Vazquez told the *Washington Post*. "I know I made a mistake. But I did it because people want to see elephants in their circus. You know what I mean."

Now that's quite a stretch, rationalizing elephant smuggling. Wouldn't you agree? But when you think about it, probably not much more of a stretch than the rationalizations we try to give on a regular basis for the things we try to smuggle into our lives without God noticing.

Most of us don't hire "coyotes" to help us since we've had so many years of practice. Just a little compromise here, a little indulgence there, a little sin wrapped up so neatly that we think we can cross the border in broad daylight and no one will ever know, especially God.

But the truth of the matter is Numbers 32:23 says, "Be careful, your sin will find you out." Someone will blow the whistle. Someone will see. Someone will find out. Somehow.

Somewhere. You'll get caught. Count on it.

We hide a lot behind the expensive suits, designer dresses, and the disarming smiles, trying to give the false impression that everything's okay when in reality we've got an elephant-sized sin we're trying to sneak by our friends, family, and fellow church members.

Take some incredibly good advice: declare what's in your life today. Confess your sin. Repent of it, renounce it, and receive forgiveness for it. Because if you don't, there's a border Guard up ahead Who's going to expose it all, and then you're really going to be in trouble.

"Nothing in all creation is hidden from God's sight. Everything is uncovered and laid bare before the eyes of him to whom we must give account" (Hebrews 4:13).

WHAT'S THE POINT?

A scandal had been brewing in Norway over the August 25, 2001, wedding of Crown Prince Haakon and his bride, Mette-Marit Tjessem Hoiby. No, it's not her name that had many Norwegians in a royal huff. It's not even the fact she was an unwed mother with a 4-year-old boy. More than half of the country's first-born children have been born to unwed mothers.

It's not the fact she was a former waitress or that she has been reported to have been involved with drugs. The father of her boy is in prison because of cocaine possession, and she had been seen at numerous parties where illegal drugs were used. It's not even the fact that Crown Prince Haakon and his bride had been living together for six months prior to the wedding. Cohabitation is routinely accepted in Norway.

So what's the big scandal? Simply this. A growing number of Norwegians are wondering out loud: "If the royal family is like everyone else, who needs them?" Political scientist Bernt Aardal said, "Being part of the royal family is not like being part of other families. You can't be above the people and be one of the people at the same time."

The scandal had widened thanks to the Crown Prince's sister, Martha, who was photographed in the company of Ari Behn, a young writer involved in questionable activities. They were both seen on Norwegian TV in the company of prostitutes, some of whom were sniffing cocaine. Behn insisted he was merely reporting on their Las Vegas lifestyle and not endorsing it or engaging in it. Still the reaction was one of outrage.

"This is just getting worse and worse," said Deputy Minister of Municipalities Einar Gelius in Norway's largest newspaper *Verdens Gang*. "First Mette-Marit Tjessem Hoiby's unrestrained partying, and now Ari Behn wading in women and dope. The monarchy is digging its own grave."

There's another royal family presently endangering their standing not only among the people of Norway but people all over the world. And this scandal is much worse and will have far greater ramifications than the Crown Prince and his bride ever imagined. This royal family is the church.

In speaking of the church the Bible says, "But you are a chosen people, a royal priesthood, a holy nation, a people belonging to God" (1 Peter 2:9). The King James Version says the church is to be a "peculiar" people. Sadly, in far too many cases the only thing peculiar about us is that we are so much like the world.

Peter went on to say, "Dear friends, I urge you, as aliens and strangers in the world, to abstain from sinful desires, which war against your soul. Live such good lives among the pagans that, though they accuse you of doing wrong, they may see your good deeds and glorify God on the day he visits us" (1 Peter 2:11-12).

If we don't, the world will look at us and say, "What's the point? Who needs them?"

HAS THE CONTEMPORARY CHURCH
BECOME A NON-PROPHET ORGANIZATION?

I was in Los Angeles when I heard the news, and I'll never forget it. It was Thursday night, March 29, 2001. A chartered jet crashed into a hillside just a few hundred yards short of the runway in Aspen, Colorado. Evidently the Gulfstream III twin turbojet reached the resort about 7 p.m. The Aspen airport is about 7800 feet up in the Rocky Mountains.

The chartered plane with 15 passengers and three crew members on board had already abandoned its initial approach and circled around in the heavy snowfall for a second attempt at landing. According to the Los Angeles Times, "Two other chartered jets—one immediately ahead of the doomed plane and one behind—also missed their first passes at the landing strip, pulling up at the last moment, several sources said. Neither risked a second try, rerouting instead to another airport as poor weather and darkness closed in."

It was reported that just after 7 p.m., the pilot had asked the tower if the runway lights were on. The tower said yes and asked if they were in sight. Six seconds later the pilot answered yes. That would be his last transmission. Moments later the plane slammed into the hillside wing first.

What makes this accident even more tragic is the fact that two days before the crash the Federal Aviation Administration had issued a warning that planes should not be allowed to make instrument landings at the Aspen airport at night. But apparently they never got it.

The flight had originated from Burbank with a brief stop in Los Angeles. According to Carol Carmody, the National Transportation Safety Board's acting chairwoman, during that brief stop the pilot had received the warning, but it was not written clearly and the pilot may not have understood it.

Consequently 18 people died completely unnecessarily. All because they didn't get the warning that could've saved their lives.

As you consider the contemporary evangelical scene, one can't help but wonder if there isn't an even greater tragedy looming on the horizon. This time the concern is not with pilots but rather with pulpits where the very warnings that could save people's lives are rarely being heard anymore.

The apostle Paul, who said, "Remember that for three years I never stopped warning each of you night and day with tears" (Acts 20:31), would be woefully out of place and awkwardly out of step in many contemporary churches where the wooing of seekers has replaced the warning of sinners.

John the Baptist, whose casual dress (to be quite honest) would fit right in with a majority of contemporary churches, would get kicked out for his convicting denunciations against sin. Using terms like "brood of vipers" and preaching about repentance won't get you many speaking engagements. In fact, it was John's preaching, especially his strong stand against the sins of the political leaders of his day, that got him beheaded.

Jonathan Edwards' famous sermon, "Sinners in the Hands of an Angry God," or R.G. Lee's "Payday Someday" wouldn't attract a very big crowd to the coffee cafe in most modern church atriums but those sermons did bring crowds of people to the altar. And their lives were saved because of it.

Paul's encouragement to Timothy, his young son in the faith, was, "In the presence of God and of Christ Jesus, who will judge the living and the dead, and in view of his appearing and his kingdom, I give you this charge: Preach the Word; be prepared in season and out of season; correct, rebuke and encourage—with great patience and careful instruction. For the time will come when men will not put up with sound doctrine" (2 Timothy 4:1-3a).

Strangely and quite unnecessarily, more often than not we may be doing more harm than good. On that Gulfstream III twin turbojet people were provided a wonderful, enjoyable ride, first-class accommodations, and the promise of a safe landing, only to have their destinies abruptly and irreversibly changed forever because they didn't get the warning they needed most.

Shouldn't we do everything we possibly can to avoid another senseless and totally unnecessary tragedy? Absolutely! But how? Simple. Preach the Word! (2 Timothy 4:1-5). Don't hold back or hesitate to proclaim the whole counsel of God! (Acts 20:27). And, finally, be a "watchman" and sound the warnings God has given in His Word (Ezekiel 33:1-9).

If we don't ... their blood will be on *our* hands.

RECOMMENDED READING

Akin, H.L. Bert. *The Pastor's Complete Guide to Personal Financial Planning*. Nashville: Nelson, 1993.

Alcorn, Randy. *Money, Possessions and Eternity*, Wheaton, IL: , 2003

————. *The Treasure Principle*, Sisters, OR: Multnomah, 2001

Bach, David. *The Automatic Millionaire*, New York: Broadway, 2004

————. *Smart Couples Finish Rich*, New York: Broadway, 2002

————. *Start Late, Finish Rich*, New York: Broadway, 2005

Barnett, Joe R. *The People Who Tested God*. Austin: Sweet Publishing, 1979.

Bell, Matt. *Money, Purpose, Joy*. Colorado Springs: NavPress, 2008.

Benna, R. Theodore, and William Proctor. *Escaping the Coming Retirement Crisis*. Colorado Springs: Piñon, 1995.

Benson, Dan. *21 Days to Financial Freedom*. Grand Rapids: Zondervan, 1998.

Berg, Jeff, and Jim Burgess. *The Debt-Free Church*. Chicago: Moody, 1996.

Blue, Ron. *The Debt Squeeze*. Pomona, CA: Focus on the Family, 1989.

————. *Generous Living*. Grand Rapids: Zondervan, 1997.

————. *Master Your Money*. Nashville: Lifeway, 1990.

————. *Money Talks, So Can We*. Grand Rapids: Zondervan, 1999.

Blue, Ron and Jeremy White. *Surviving Financial Meltdown*. Carol Stream, IL: Tyndale, 2009.

Blue, Ron and Judy. *Money Matters for Parents and Their Kids*. Nashville: Oliver Nelson, 1988.

Burkett, Larry. *The Complete Financial Guide for Young Couples*. Wheaton, IL: Victor, 1989.

————. *The Complete Guide to Managing Your Money*. New York: Inspirational Press, 1996.

————. *Debt Free Investing*. Chicago: Moody, 1995.

————. *Debt-Free Living*. Chicago: Moody, 1989.

_____. *Dollars and $ense*. Uhrichsville, OH: Barbour, 1997.

_____. *The Financial Guide for the Single Parent*. Chicago: Moody, 1997.

_____. *Financial Parenting*. Colorado Springs: Chariot Victor, 1996.

_____. *Money before Marriage*. Chicago: Moody, 1996.

_____. *Money in Marriage*. Chicago: Moody, 1999.

_____. *Investing for the Future*. Wheaton, IL: Victor, 1992.

_____. *Preparing for Retirement*. Chicago: Moody, 1992.

_____. *Using Your Money Wisely*. Chicago: Moody, 1985.

_____. *Women Leaving the Workplace*. Chicago: Moody, 1995.

_____. *The Word on Finances*. Chicago: Moody, 1994.

_____. *Your Child and Money*. Chicago: Moody, 2000.

_____. *Your Complete Guide to Financial Security*. New York: Inspirational Press, 1992.

_____. *What The Bible Says About Money*. Brentwood, TN: Wolgemuth & Hyatt, 1989.

_____. *Business by the Book*. Nashville: Thomas Nelson, 1990.

_____. *Answers to Your Family's Financial Questions*. Pomona, CA: Focus on the Family, 1987.

_____. *Whatever Happened to the American Dream*. Chicago: Moody, 1993.

_____. *The Coming Economic Earthquake*. Chicago: Moody, 1991.

Burkett, Larry and Ron Blue. *Wealth to Last*. Nashville: Broadman/Holman, 2003.

Dayton, Howard. *Your Money Map*, Chicago: Moody, 2006.

Dollar, Truman. *How to Carry Out God's Stewardship Plan*. Nashville: Nelson, 1974.

Eisenberg, Lee. *The Number*, New York: Free Press, 2006

Eisenson, Marc. *The Banker's Secret*. New York: Villard, 1984.

Eker, T. Harv. *Secrets of the Millionaire Mind*, New York: Harper, 2005

Getz, Dr. Gene. *Rich in Every Way*, West Monroe, LA: Howard, 2004

Gotthardt, Alan. *The Eternity Portfolio*. Wheaton, IL: Tyndale, 2003.

Hagee, John. *Financial Armageddon.* Lake Mary, FL: Strang Communications, 2008.

Howard, Alton. *Money Grows on Trees.* West Monroe, LA: Howard, 1994.

Hunt, Mary. *Debt-Proof Living.* Nashville: Broadman/Holman, 1999.

_____. *Debt-Proof Your Kids.* Nashville: Broadman/Holman, 1998.

_____. *Live Your Life for Half the Price,* Los Angeles: DPL Press, 2005

Jeavons, Thomas H. and Rebekah Burch Basinger. *Growing Givers' Hearts,* San Francisco: Jossey-Bass, 1995

Jeremiah, Dr. David. *The Coming Economic Armageddon.* New York: Faith Words, 2010.

Johnson, Stacy. *Life or Debt.* New York: Ballantine, 2002.

Kiyosaki, Robert T. *The Cashflow Quadrant.* New York: Warner Books, 1998.

_____. *Rich Dad, Poor Dad.* New York: Warner Books, 1997.

_____. *Rich Kid, Smart Kid.* New York: Warner Books, 2000.

Lapin, Rabbi Daniel. *Thou Shall Prosper.* Hoboken, NJ: Wiley, 2002.

Lloyd, Nancy. *Simple Money Solutions.* New York: Random House, 2000.

MacArthur, John. *Whose Money Is It, Anyway?* Nashville: Word, 2000.

Miller, Peter G. *The Common Sense Mortgage.* New York: Harper & Row, 1987.

Moore, Gary. *Ten Golden Rules for Financial Success,* Grand Rapids, MI: Zondervan, 1996

Nowery, Kirk. *The Giving Church.* Camarillo, CA: Spire, 2006.

_____. *360° Stewardship.* Camarillo, CA: Spire, 2007.

Olford, Stephen. *The Grace of Giving.* Grand Rapids: Kregel, 2000.

Orman, Suze. *The Courage to Be Rich.* New York: Riverhead, 1999.

_____. *The Laws of Money, The Lessons of Life,* New York: Free Press, 2003

_____. *The Money Book for the Young, Fabulous & Broke,* New York: Riverhead, 2005

_____. *The 9 Steps to Financial Freedom.* New York: Crown, 1997.

Paris, James L. *Financial Boot Camp*. Lake Mary, FL: Creation House, 1992.

Pilzer, Paul Zane. *God Wants You to Be Rich*. New York: Fireside, 1997.

Pollan, Stephen M., and Mark Levine. *Live Rich*. New York: Harper Business, 1998.

Ramsey, Dave. *Financial Peace*. New York: Viking, 1997.

_____. *How to Have More Than Enough*. New York: Penguin, 2000.

_____. *More Than Enough*. New York: Viking, 1997.

_____. *Priceless*. Nashville: Countryman, 2002.

_____. *The Total Money Makeover*. Nashville: Thomas Nelson, 2003.

Ramsey, Dave and Rachel Cruze. *Smart Money, Smart Kids*. Brentwood, TN: Lampo, 2014.

Reynard, Michael. *Money Secrets of the Rich and Famous*. New York: Allworth Press, 1999.

Russell, Bob. *Money: A User's Manual*. Sisters, OR: Multnomah, 1997.

Searcy, Nelson. *the generosity ladder*. Grand Rapids: Baker, 2010.

_____. *maximize*. Grand Rapids: Baker, 2010.

Stanley, Andy. *Fields of Gold*, Wheaton, IL: Tyndale, 2004.

Stanley, Thomas. *The Millionaire Mind*. Kansas City, MO: Andrews McMeel, 2000.

_____. *The Millionaire Next Door*. Marietta, GA: Longstreet Press, 1996.

Stovall, Jim and Tim Maurer. *The Ultimate Financial Plan*. Hoboken, NJ: Wiley, 2011.

Taylor, Jack R. *God's Miraculous Plan of Economy*. Nashville: Broadman, 1975.

Temple, Todd. *Money: How to Make It, Spend It and Keep Lots of It*. Nashville: Broadman/Holman, 1998.

Warren, Elizabeth and Amelia Warren Tyagi. *All Your Worth*. NY: Free Press, 2005.

Watts, Wayne. *The Gift of Giving*. Colorado Springs: NavPress, 1982.

Wilkinson, Bruce. *The God Pocket*, Colorado Springs: Multnomah, 2011.

CONTAGIOUS GENEROSITY
by Barry L. Cameron

Generosity is contagious! Several years ago, thanks to the generosity of some dear friends, I was privileged to stay at the historic, world-class, 3,000-acre resort in Colorado Springs, Colorado, called *The Broadmoor*. Its breathtaking, Italian Renaissance styled buildings and grounds are nestled at the base of Cheyenne Mountain, with the picture-perfect backdrop of the Rocky Mountains and Pike's Peak. We had flown in from Texas, and when we checked in, the suite our friends had reserved wasn't available. No problem for the folks at the Broadmoor. They generously upgraded us to a larger suite. We checked into our room, and I stood on the balcony, soaking it all in, staring in awe at the most gorgeous scenery I had ever seen in my life. I was more in awe that, thanks to our friends, we were the recipients of such unbelievable generosity; and my experience with the generosity of the Broadmoor was just beginning.

A few minutes later as I tried to unpack my suitcase, I discovered the baggage handlers at the airport had messed up the lock on my bag, and there was no way I was going to get it open. I tried to find a local business that carried Samsonite luggage. The closest one was about an hour away. I phoned my friend; he told me to call the concierge to see if he could help. Sure enough, he told me to leave my bag in the room and he would handle it.

We left to do some sightseeing. When we returned, my bag was open on the bed with a note from the concierge thanking me for giving him the privilege to help me. When I called to offer to pay for this kindness he told me again it was his privilege to help and to call if there was anything else I needed. Later on I inquired to find out what had been done to get my bag fixed and learned the concierge had sent someone to the luggage dealer we had found an hour away. I was blown away by their generosity and still am.

My wife and I were overwhelmed by the generosity of our friends and the generosity of the Broadmoor. So, a few years later, when we had paid off the mortgage on our home and gotten out of debt, we invited two more of our friends to go with us to the Broadmoor. We told them we would pay for everything, including plane flights, rooms, and rental car. This time they would be the recipients of our generosity. It was an incredible experience for all of us and reinforced the principle that "it is more blessed to give than it is to receive" (Acts 20:35), because we received a greater blessing from giving generously to our friends than we did being the recipients of others' generosity to us. My wife and I have made it a regular habit to try to go to the Broadmoor at least once a year. In fact, the idea for this book and the initial chapters were written while we were staying at the Broadmoor.

Generosity is always contagious and is supposed to be a normal way of life for all of us. Not just an occasional experience reserved for those who visit a nice resort. How do I know? Because that's the way the Creator of the Universe designed us, and everything in our world—to be generous.

You and I weren't created to keep anything. We were created to give and to give generously. However, every study conducted concerning the giving habits of people in our world comes back with the same results: we're experts at keeping, but novices when it comes to giving. An article in the *New York*

Times (December, 2005) had the headline: "Study Shows the Superrich Are Not the Most Generous." The article stated that the more money we make, the less generous we are. Respected Christian research expert, George Barna, says that even though evangelical Christians are among the most generous givers of all, less than 10% of them tithe to their local church.

What does all that tell us? It means we're great keepers, but not so great givers. All of us. And the shocking reality is that those of us inside the church apparently struggle just as much with selfishness as our unchurched counterparts. Embarrassing as it may be, research clearly shows the contemporary evangelical community, as a whole, is not good at giving. And you really can't call us generous.

Do you see the problem? God does. After all, He created us. You and I weren't created to keep anything. We were created to give—everything.

Hold It.

Don't believe me? Try keeping your next breath. You weren't created to keep it. You were created to give it. If you don't believe me, just try to keep it. You can't. Go ahead and hold your next breath. Try to keep it. I'll wait on you. While you're doing that, look at your watch and count the seconds as it becomes uncomfortable.

How did I know you were going to start feeling uncomfortable holding your breath? Because you weren't created to keep it. None of us were. You were created to receive that breath and then to give it back—you were not created to keep it. You and I weren't created to keep anything. We were created to give. We were created not just to give, but also to be generous with everything—including the air we breathe. God never intended for any of us to be keepers. He created us to give, and to give generously.

Now, if you or someone else decides no matter what anyone else says, you're going to keep your next breath, do you understand what will eventually happen? In fact, "eventually" won't be very long in coming. It will be more like four to six minutes at the max. If you attempt to hold that breath and don't give it back—you'll die. Know why? Because you weren't created to keep it. You were created to give. When you keep instead of giving, you are going to die. It's inevitable. It's inescapable.

The Creator of the universe, Almighty God, created everything in the universe (which includes you and me) to give and not to keep, to be generous and not selfish.

Let me share with you an incredible principle right up front: selfishness is destructive and deadly. It always maims, always steals, always kills, and always destroys. Always. On the other hand, generosity always blesses, always increases, always brings life, and always brings abundance. Always. That's why God created everything to give and not to keep. He's a God of giving, a God of life, and a God of continuous blessing.

So if you want to be blessed continuously, what do you think you need to do? Give and give generously. Generous giving, like generous breathing, will always bring continuous blessing—the blessing of life. Trying to keep instead (like trying to hold your breath) won't lengthen or strengthen your life. Quite the opposite, keeping always leads to death. Keeping actually takes blessings away from us, while giving brings blessings to us. It's counterintuitive, as many of the most life-transforming spiritual principles are.

In Luke 9:24, Jesus said, "For whoever wants to save his life will lose it, but whoever loses his life for me will save it." In Matthew 20:26, He said, "Whoever wants to become great among you must be your servant." In His most famous sermon, the Sermon on the Mount, Jesus told His disciples to "love your enemies and pray for those who persecute you" (Matthew 5:44).

Take a drink.

Here's another test for you. Get a glass of water and take a drink. In fact, drink all the water in the glass. Now, here's your assignment: try to keep it. Okay, I'll admit you can keep the water longer than you did the breath you tried to keep. But even though you can go several hours and maybe even a day or two, eventually you won't be able to keep that drink of water. Know why? Because you weren't designed to keep it. God designed you and me to receive a drink of water and enjoy it. One drink can nourish our thirst and satisfy us. But the satisfaction is temporary because God didn't create us to keep it. In a matter of hours, sometimes only minutes, we'll be thirsty again. Our body takes the water in and then passes the water out. Our needs are met in the process, but we are not allowed to keep the water. Why? **Because we weren't created to be keepers. We were created to be givers.**

Now, I want to stretch your brain a little. Do you realize that since the original seven days of creation, God has not created anything new? Check it out, and you'll find it to be true. God did all of His creative work in those six consecutive days and then, on the seventh day, He rested. What that means is that God created all the air the world would ever need and all the water the world would ever need in those six days of creation. That means you and I and every person who has ever lived on this earth have been breathing the same air and drinking the same water God created during those original six days of creation. God was the One Who came up with recycling. Long before man ever came up with those green recycling containers, God had already initiated the world's first and foremost recycling program.

Now you can understand why God created us the way He did. He created us to be generous and to be givers rather than keepers. If those who lived before us had been keepers instead of givers, you and I wouldn't have any air to breathe or any water to drink. Think about that for a moment. All of us are absolutely and completely codependent on the generosity of others to live. God designed the universe and placed resources there that could be used over and over again. That's why they're called re-sources. Wow! Do you understand the implications of that statement? If others weren't willing to share with us and be generous with basic necessities like air and water, we couldn't live. Likewise, if you and I are unwilling to be generous and share with others, others will inevitably die as well.

Let me give you another example. Remember the last restaurant where you ate? Do you realize that restaurant and every other restaurant on earth was built to be generous and to give but never to keep? Granted, God didn't create those restaurants, men did. But the principle of contagious generosity is built into every fiber of our universe, even our eating establishments. For instance, every restaurant on the earth receives food and gives food. That's why they're in business. They are not in business to keep food. If they try to keep it, they'll go out of business. The owner would go broke because he's in business to give.

I am fully aware it sounds weird when you read it. But it's true. That's how a restaurant owner makes money—by giving. He doesn't make a dime by keeping. If he doesn't provide food for his customers, he won't have any customers, certainly no paying customers. But it goes way beyond that.

For example, if that restaurant receives a delivery of fresh bread and they decide they want to keep the bread instead of give it, what will happen? Instead of giving fresh bread to their customers who come in to eat, if they decide they want to keep that bread on the shelves, what do you think will happen to that bread? You're already ahead of me, aren't you? That bread is going to spoil, mold, and rot until it becomes obvious to everyone it has to be thrown away. Who in their right mind would keep perfectly good bread on a shelf until it becomes no good for anyone, including the person who made the decision to keep it?

In case you ever wondered why there are dates on boxes of cereal and crackers, bottles of orange juice and milk, cartons of butter and jars of mayonnaise, the reason is simple. If those items are kept beyond the date stamped on the package or container, they start to go bad and are of no use to anyone. In fact, the consumption of any of those items beyond the date given would be very unwise and could quite possibly be hazardous to your health.

You've probably heard the phrase "shelf life" used in reference to food. Truth is, the phrase is actually contradictory. Nothing has a shelf life. If something stays on a shelf, it's already dying. It would be more accurate to speak of the "shelf death" of things rather than their "shelf life." Every item in a grocery store or restaurant is designed to be given, not kept. Whether you're talking about grocery stores, restaurants, or even cars, the principle of contagious generosity is built into every aspect of our universe.

When it comes to your finances, you deserve the wisdom of Solomon.

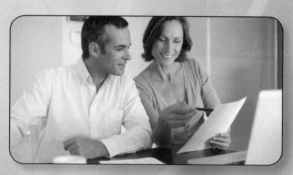

When you invest with The Solomon Foundation, you not only get excellent interest rates, you are providing the funding for the future expansion and growth of the Restoration Movement Christian Church and Churches of Christ all across America.

With flexible terms, excellent interest rates, and offerings for every budget, The Solomon Foundation has the right investment vehicle to reach your financial goals.

Learn how you can be a vital part of this ministry through the various investment and loan opportunities.

Call today (855) 873-5873

Excellent Interest. Eternal Impact.

thesolomonfoundation.org

NOW AVAILABLE IN SPANISH

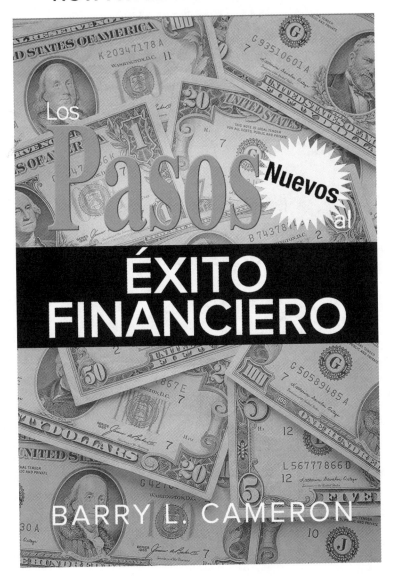

Los **Pasos** *Nuevos* al

ÉXITO FINANCIERO

BARRY L. CAMERON

Available at *The Disciple Shop* bookstore at Crossroads
toll free: (888) 360-7648

THE FINANCIAL FREEDOM WORKBOOK

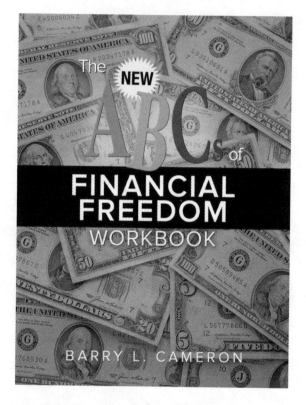

The Financial Freedom Workbook is a tremendous tool to help you get on the road to financial freedom. This 6-week study (perfect for small groups or individuals) will help you learn how to achieve complete financial freedom, pay off all your debts early, develop a simple, useable budget, find money you didn't know you had to put in savings each week, and how you can live a debt-free life and pass it on to your children.

CONTAGIOUS GENEROSITY
The Key To Continuous Blessing!

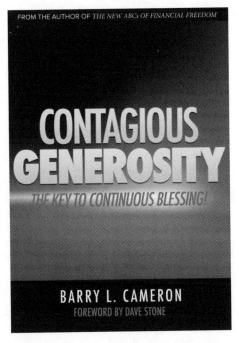

"If you were blessed by Barry's first book, *The ABCs of Financial Freedom*, you'll be blessed even more by *Contagious Generosity*."

"Wow! What a great book! Barry Cameron has given us, in *Contagious Generosity*, a clarion call to discover the joy and fulfillment of becoming and being God's agents of blessing to others."

"Get ready to be surprised, challenged, and inspired. Practicing these principles will not only change your life, but change our world for the better."

"Barry Cameron practices what he preaches. I have watched Barry and the congregation he serves live out their commitment to contagious generosity."

Available at *The Disciple Shop* bookstore at Crossroads
toll free: (888) 360-7648

To contact the author:
Barry L. Cameron, Senior Pastor
Crossroads Christian Church
6450 S. State Highway 360
Grand Prairie, TX 75052
or
http://www.crossroadschristian.org

To read Barry's blog each week:
http://www.crossroadschristian.org/blog/

Follow Barry on

barry.cameron.399

@BarryLCameron

@BarryLCameron

linkedin.com/pub/barry-cameron/32/538/6aa